WHAT'S COOKI

Indian

Shehzad Husain

This edition published by Parragon, 1999
Parragon
Queen Street House
4 Queen Street
Bath BA1 1HE

ISBN: 0-75252-938-2 (paperback)
ISBN: 0-75253-234-0 (hardback)

Printed in Indonesia

Produced by Haldane Mason, London

Acknowledgements
Art Director: Ron Samuels
Editorial Director: Sydney Francis
Editorial Consultant: Christopher Fagg
Managing Editor: Jo-Anne Cox
Design: Digital Artworks Partnership Ltd
Photography: Iain Bagwell
Home Economist: Penny Stephens
Home Economist's Assistants: Nicky Deeley, Sarwat Jehan, Jean Stephens

Note
Cup measurements in this book are for American cups.
Tablespoons are assumed to be 15 ml. Unless otherwise stated,
milk is assumed to be full fat, eggs are size 3
and pepper is freshly ground black pepper.

Contents

Introduction

The subcontinent of India and Pakistan covers some 4 million square kilometres and comprises very many different cultures and religions, of which the main groups are the Hindus and Muslims, within each of which are smaller sects, the Parsees and the Christians. All of these have influenced the eating habits and tastes of the various ethnic communities throughout the subcontinent. The food eaten in the north, for example, differs considerably from that of the south. The people of the north, which is a wheat-growing area, prefer Indian breads such as *chapatis* or *paratas* as their staple, while rice which is grown in many of the southern states is preferred by the southerners.

Muslims are the meat-eating population of India, but for religious reasons they do not eat anything derived from the pig, which is considered unclean. Hindus, a vast majority of whom are vegetarians, are forbidden to eat beef, because the cow is considered a sacred animal.

Spices and herbs have been used to flavour food for thousands of years in the East, and India has for centuries been an important source of spices for Western nations. Yet it is only in the last twenty years or so that the majority of people in the West have become generally aware of our spicy cuisine. This may well be due in part to the great ease of communication, by jet travel, with India, and the fact that many people are now travelling to the Indian subcontinent where they have the opportunity to taste a variety of dishes on their home ground. But most of all it has been due to the proliferation of Indian restaurants in towns and cities throughout the world and, in particular, the British Isles. The Indian communities which have settled in Britain and in other countries have not only preserved their own culture and eating habits but, through setting up their own trading systems for specialist ingredients, made real Indian cookery possible on a far wider scale than would have been thought possible even, say, ten years ago.

Indian dishes are wonderfully good-tempered, in that very few of them need any last minute attention whatsoever (maybe just sprinkling with a garnish in some cases); the majority of the dishes can be made well in advance and will freeze successfully – and indeed, some actually improve through keeping; others will usually keep in a refrigerator for a day or so until you are ready to reheat them; this means that the cook, provided he/she has planned his/her meal carefully, can join his/her guests for a drink before the meal without the slightest worry about what might be happening in the kitchen. Also, because it is perfectly correct to serve all the dishes, other than dessert, at once, he/she need not leap up from the first course in order to get the main course organised – everything can go on the table at the beginning of the meal.

What about the question of spiciness? Must you spend a fortune on a cupboard full of exotic items before you even begin? And how do you gauge what degree of 'hotness' will be acceptable to your guests? Almost all the recipes in this book contain spices of one sort or another, but not necessarily a wide selection for each individual dish. Some curries, for example, require just two types of spice, another might need a combination of, say, twelve different herbs and spices. However, if you know you like Indian food and are likely to be cooking it on a regular basis, it is advisable to buy a basic range of spices for your own convenience (see Store-cupboard Items, opposite) which will see you through a good variety of recipes. Then build up gradually as you start to try others. Hotness often depends on the amount of chilli, in whatever form: fresh chillies, which I use a great deal for garnish as well as in curry sauces, dried chillies and ground chilli (chilli powder also known as cayenne pepper). It is well to under-rather than over-estimate the amount of chilli you will need until you gain some experience in Indian cooking, and to remember that you can take some of the sting out of chilli pods by scraping out the seeds. But, most importantly, do not make the mistake of thinking that all Indian curries must be red-hot to be 'authentic' They need not be, and moreover we usually serve a variety of mild and hot dishes at any given meal. You should always plan your meals to include both milder and hotter dishes, because there is no point in destroying your guests' palates for your more delicately-flavoured dishes by killing their taste buds with chilli.

EQUIPMENT FOR INDIAN COOKING

Your own kitchen will probably be equipped already with everything needed for cooking a full range of Indian dishes. Some good-quality saucepans, with thick bases, and a heavy-bottomed frying-pan (skillet) are essential, and you will want some wooden spatulas and, ideally, a perforated spoon for stirring rice, to use with them. You will want at least one good, sharp knife and for measuring some spoons and a jug. Kitchen scales could be helpful, too.

For grinding spices you can use a pestle and mortar, a coffee grinder or food processor, or a rolling-pin: in many Indian households a flat, heavy grindstone and something like a rolling-pin (called a *mussal*) are still considered the best solution. Some people find a garlic press useful, too, for Indian cookery.

STORE-CUPBOARD ITEMS

Your basic stock of spices should include fresh ginger and garlic, chilli powder, turmeric, cardamom, black pepper, ground coriander and cumin. The powdered spices will keep very well in airtight containers, carefully labelled, while the fresh ginger and garlic will keep for 7-10 days in the

refrigerator. Other useful items, to be acquired as your repertoire increases, are cumin seeds (black as well as white), onion seeds, mustard seeds, cloves, cinnamon, dried red chillies, fenugreek, vegetable ghee and garam masala (a mixture of spices that can either be bought ready-made or home-made in quantity for use whenever required. Tomato purée (paste) is also useful.

USING SPICES

There are many ways of using spices. You can use them whole, ground, roasted, fried, or mixed with yogurt to marinate meat and poultry. One spice can alter the flavour of a dish and a combination of several can produce different colours and textures.

The quantities of spices shown in the recipes in this book are merely a guide. Do not hesitate to increase or decrease them as you wish, especially in the cases of salt and chilli powder, which are very much a matter of taste.

Many of the recipes in this book call for ground spices, which are generally available in supermarkets as well as in Indian and Pakistani grocers. In India we almost always buy whole spices and grind them ourselves, and there is no doubt that freshly ground spices do make a noticeable difference to the taste. However, there is no denying that it is more convenient, and quicker, to use ground spices.

For some of the recipes in this book, the spices need to be roasted. In India this is done on a *thawa*, but you can use a heavy, ideally cast iron frying-pan (skillet). No water or oil is added to the spices: they are simply dry-roasted whole while the pan is shaken to stop them burning.

Remember that long cooking over a lowish heat will improve the taste of the food as it allows the spices to be absorbed. This is why re-heating the following day is no problem for most Indian food. Do feel free to experiment: only you know how you want your food to taste.

Meat & Fish

There is a wide variety of meat recipes in this chapter, and in most cases the meat is lamb. I prefer to use leg of lamb, as it is much less fatter than shoulder, but if you like shoulder I suggest you combine it with an equal proportion of leg, which works very well. In some of the recipes beef (braising steak, for example) may be substituted for lamb, but if you do this you will need to allow a little extra cooking time.

In India, chicken is expensive and is therefore considered a special-occasion meat. A chicken dish is invariably served at every function. Indians always cook chicken skinned and cut into small pieces. If the chicken weighs about 1.5 kg/3 lb 5 oz it should be cut into about 8 pieces, unless you are making Tandoori Chicken, when chicken quarters look a lot better and are more appropriate. Ask you local butcher to skin, cut and bone the chicken for you if required.

India may not be thought of as a great fish-eating nation, but there are certain parts of it, notably Bengal and around the city of Karachi, where fish is very popular. Indeed, the staple diet of the Bengalis is fish and rice; they enjoy river fish from the Hooghli and also lobster and king prawns (shrimp).

Hot Spicy Lamb in Sauce

This North Indian dish is traditionally served for a late breakfast or brunch. Ideally it should be cooked all night and served in the morning with naan bread, but it can be cooked the day before and re-heated.

Serves 6-8

INGREDIENTS

175 ml/6 fl oz/³/4 cup oil
1 kg/2 lb 4 oz lean leg of lamb, cut
   into large pieces
1 tbsp ground garam masala
5 medium onions, chopped
150 ml/5 fl oz/²/3 cup yogurt
2 tbsp tomato purée (paste)
2 tsp fresh ginger root, finely
   chopped

2 tsp fresh garlic, crushed
1¹/2 tsp salt
2 tsp chilli powder
1 tbsp ground coriander
2 tsp ground nutmeg
900 ml/1¹/2 pints/3³/4 cups water
1 tbsp ground fennel seeds
1 tbsp paprika
1 tbsp *bhoonay chanay* or gram flour

3 bay leaves
1 tbsp plain (all-purpose) flour
naan breads or paratas, to serve

TO GARNISH:
2-3 green chillies, chopped
fresh coriander (cilantro) leaves,
   chopped

1 Heat the oil in a pan and add the meat and half of the garam masala. Stir-fry the mixture for 7-10 minutes until the meat is well coated. Using a perforated spoon, remove the meat and set aside.

2 Add the onions to the pan and fry until golden brown. Return the meat to the pan, reduce the heat and leave to simmer, stirring occasionally.

3 In a separate bowl, mix the yogurt and tomato purée (paste), ginger, garlic, salt, chilli powder, ground coriander, nutmeg and the rest of the garam masala. Pour this mixture over the meat and stir-fry, mixing the spices well into the meat, for 5-7 minutes.

4 Add half of the water, then the fennel, paprika and *bhoonay chanay* or gram flour. Add the remaining water and the bay leaves, lower the heat, cover and cook for 1 hour, stirring.

5 Mix the flour in 2 tbsp of warm water and pour this mixture over the curry. Garnish with the chillies and the coriander (cilantro) and cook until the meat is tender and the sauce thickens. Serve with Naan Bread (see page 178) or Paratas (see page 174).

Tomatoes Cooked with Meat & Yogurt

One of my favourites, this delicious tomato khorma *has a
semi-thick sauce. I like to serve freshly made Chapatis (see page 180) with it.*

Serves 2-4

INGREDIENTS

1 tsp garam masala
1 tsp fresh ginger root, finely
    chopped
1 tsp fresh garlic, crushed
2 black cardamoms
1 tsp chilli powder
$^1/_2$ tsp black cumin seeds

2 x 2.5 cm/1-inch cinnamon sticks
1 tsp salt
150 ml/5 fl oz/$^2/_3$ cup natural yogurt
$^1/_2$ kg/1 lb 2 oz lean cubed lamb
150 ml/$^1/_4$ pint/$^2/_3$ cup oil
2 onions, sliced
600 ml/1 pint/2$^1/_2$ cups water

2 firm tomatoes, cut into quarters
2 tbsp lemon juice

TO GARNISH:
fresh coriander (cilantro) leaves,
    chopped
2 green chillies, chopped

1 In a large mixing bowl, mix together the garam masala, ginger, garlic, cardamoms, chilli powder, black cumin seeds, cinnamon sticks, salt and the yogurt until well combined.

2 Add the meat to the yogurt and spice mixture and mix well to coat the meat. Set aside.

3 Heat the oil in a large saucepan and fry the onions until golden brown.

4 Add the meat to the pan and stir-fry for about 5 minutes. Reduce the heat, add the water, cover the pan and simmer for about 1 hour, stirring occasionally.

5 Add the tomatoes to the curry and sprinkle with the lemon juice. Leave the curry to simmer for a further 7-10 minutes.

6 Garnish the curry with the coriander (cilantro) leaves and the green chillies, and serve hot.

COOK'S TIP

Khormas are slowly braised dishes, many of which are the rich and spicy, Persian-inspired Mogul dishes served on special occasions. Yogurt is often featured, both as a marinade and as the cooking liquid.

In a properly cooked khorma, *prime, tender cuts of meat are used, and the small amout of cooking liquid is absorbed back into the meat to produce a succulent result.*

Lamb with Onions & Dried Mango Powder

This dish originates from Hyderabad, in central southern India.

Serves 4

INGREDIENTS

4 medium onions
300 ml/^{1}/$_2$ pint/1^1/$_4$ cups oil
1 tsp fresh ginger root, finely
   chopped
1 tsp fresh garlic, crushed

1 tsp chilli powder
1 pinch turmeric
1 tsp salt
3 green chillies
450 g/1 lb leg of lamb, cubed

600 ml/1 pint/2^1/$_2$ cups water
1^1/$_2$ tsp *aamchoor* (dried mango
   powder)
fresh coriander (cilantro) leaves

1 Using a sharp knife, chop 3 onions finely.

2 Heat 150 ml/^{1}/$_4$ pint/^{2}/$_3$ cup of the oil in a pan and fry the onions until golden brown. Reduce the heat and add the ginger, garlic, chilli powder, turmeric and salt to the pan. Stir-fry the mixture for about 5 minutes, then add 2 of the chillies.

3 Add the meat to the pan and stir-fry the mixture for a further 7 minutes.

4 Add the water to the pan, cover and cook over a low heat for 35-45 minutes, stirring occasionally.

5 Meanwhile, slice the remaining onion. Heat the remaining oil in a pan and fry the onion until golden. Set aside.

6 Once the meat is tender, add the *aamchoor* (dried mango powder), the remaining green chilli and fresh coriander (cilantro) leaves and stir-fry for 3-5 minutes.

7 Transfer the curry to a serving dish and pour the fried onion slices and oil along the centre. Serve hot.

COOK'S TIP

Aamchoor *(dried mango powder)*
is made from dried raw mangoes.
It has a sour taste and can
be bought in jars.

Lamb Pot Roast

I have always found this dish to be a great success at dinner parties, when I usually serve it with Vegetable Rice (see page 162) and Potatoes with Spices & Onions (see page 108).

Serves 6

INGREDIENTS

2.5 kg/5 lb 8 oz leg of lamb
2 tsp fresh ginger root, finely
   chopped
2 tsp fresh garlic, crushed
2 tsp garam masala
1 tsp salt

2 tsp black cumin seeds
4 black peppercorns
3 cloves
1 tsp chilli powder
3 tbsp lemon juice
300 ml/$\frac{1}{2}$ pint/$1\frac{1}{4}$ cups oil

1 large onion, peeled
about 2 litres/4 pints/10 cups water

1 Remove the fat from the lamb. Prick the lamb all over with a fork.

2 In a bowl, mix the ginger, garlic, garam masala, salt, black cumin seeds, peppercorns, cloves and chilli powder until well combined. Stir in the lemon juice and mix well. Rub the mixture all over the leg of lamb and set aside.

3 Heat the oil in a pan. Add the meat to the pan and place the onion alongside the leg of lamb.

4 Add enough water to cover the meat and cook over a low heat for 2$\frac{1}{2}$-3 hours, turning occasionally. (If after a while the water has evaporated and the meat is not tender, add a little extra water.) Once the water has completely evaporated, turn the roast over to brown it on all sides.

5 Remove the roast from the pan and transfer to a serving dish. Cut the roast into slices or serve it whole to be carved at the table. Serve hot or cold.

COOK'S TIP

Traditionally, a pan called a degchi is used for pot-roasting in India. It is set over hot ashes and contains hot coals in its lid.

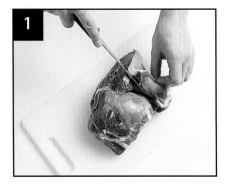

Grilled Minced Lamb

This is rather an unusual way of cooking mince. In India this is cooked on a naked flame, but I use my grill (broiler) instead and find it works just as well.

Serves 4

INGREDIENTS

5 tbsp oil
2 onions, sliced
450 g/1 lb minced lamb
2 tbsp yogurt
1 tsp chilli powder
1 tsp fresh ginger root, finely
  chopped

1 tsp fresh garlic, crushed
1 tsp salt
1¹/₂ tsp garam masala
¹/₂ tsp ground allspice
2 fresh green chillies
fresh coriander (cilantro) leaves

TO GARNISH:
1 onion, cut into rings
fresh coriander (cilantro) leaves,
  chopped
1 lemon, cut into wedges

1 Heat the oil in a saucepan. Add the onions and fry until golden brown.

2 Place the minced lamb in a large bowl. Add the yogurt, chilli powder, ginger, garlic, salt, garam masala, ground allspice and mix to combine.

3 Add the lamb mixture to the fried onions and stir-fry for 10-15 minutes. Remove from the heat and set aside.

4 Meanwhile, place the green chillies and half of the coriander (cilantro) leaves in a processor and grind. Alternatively, finely chop the green chillies and coriander (cilantro) with a sharp knife. Set aside until required.

5 Put the minced lamb mixture in a food processor and grind. Alternatively, place in a large bowl and mash with a fork. Mix the lamb mixture with the chillies and coriander (cilantro) and blend well.

6 Transfer the mixture to a shallow heatproof dish. Cook under a preheated medium-hot grill (broiler) for 10-15 minutes, moving the mixture about with a fork. Watch it carefully to prevent it from burning.

7 Serve garnished with onion rings, coriander (cilantro) and lemon wedges.

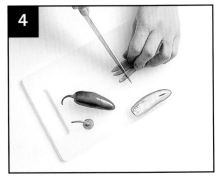

Minced Lamb with Peas

Served with a dhaal *and rice, this simple dish makes a well-balanced meal.*

Serves 4

INGREDIENTS

1 medium onion
6 tbsp oil
3 green chillies
fresh coriander (cilantro) leaves

2 tomatoes, chopped
1 tsp salt
1 tsp fresh ginger root, finely
  chopped
1 tsp fresh garlic, crushed

1 tsp chilli powder
450 g/1 lb lean minced lamb
100 g/3$^{1}/_{2}$ oz peas

1 Peel and slice the onion, using a sharp knife.

2 Heat the oil in a medium-sized saucepan. Add the onion slices and fry until golden brown, stirring.

3 Add two of the green chillies, half of the fresh coriander (cilantro) leaves and the chopped tomatoes to the pan and reduce the heat to a simmer.

4 Add the salt, ginger, garlic and chilli powder to the mixture in the pan and stir well to combine.

5 Add the minced lamb to the pan and stir-fry the mixture for 7-10 minutes.

6 Add the peas to the mixture in the pan and cook for a further 3-4 minutes, stirring occasionally.

7 Transfer the lamb and pea mixture to warm serving plates and garnish with the remaining green chilli and the fresh coriander (cilantro) leaves.

COOK'S TIP

The flavour of garlic can be changed according to how it is prepared. For instance, a whole garlic clove added to a dish will give it the flavour but not the 'bite' of garlic; a halved clove will add a little bite while a finely chopped garlic clove will release most of the flavour and a crushed clove will release all of the flavour.

Lamb Curry in a Thick Sauce

Originally a Kashmiri dish, this lamb stew is now made all over India and is popular wherever Indian food is eaten. Noted for its delicious tomato-flavoured sauce, it is ideal for a dinner party.

Serves 6

INGREDIENTS

1 kg/2 lb 4 oz lean lamb, with or without bone
7 tbsp yogurt
75 g/2^3/4 oz/5 tbsp almonds
2 tsp garam masala
2 tsp fresh ginger root, finely chopped

2 tsp fresh garlic, crushed
1^1/2 tsp chilli powder
1^1/2 tsp salt
300 ml/^{1}/2 pint/1^1/4 cups oil
3 onions, finely chopped
4 green cardamoms

2 bay leaves
3 green chillies, chopped
2 tbsp lemon juice
400 g/14 oz can tomatoes
300 ml/^{1}/2 pint/1^1/4 cups water
fresh coriander (cilantro) leaves, chopped

1 Using a very sharp knife, cut the lamb into small, even-sized pieces.

2 In a large mixing bowl, combine the yogurt, almonds, garam masala, ginger, garlic, chilli powder and salt, stirring to mix well.

3 Heat the oil in a large saucepan and fry the onions with the cardamoms and the bay leaves until golden brown, stirring constantly.

4 Add the meat and the yogurt mixture to the pan and stir-fry for 3-5 minutes.

5 Add 2 green chillies, the lemon juice and the canned tomatoes to the mixture in the pan and stir-fry for a further 5 minutes.

6 Add the water to the pan, cover and leave to simmer over a low heat for 35-40 minutes.

7 Add the remaining green chilli and the coriander (cilantro) leaves and stir until the sauce has thickened. (Remove the lid and turn the heat higher if the sauce is too watery.)

8 Transfer the curry to warm serving plates and serve hot.

Potatoes Cooked with Meat & Yogurt

Khormas almost always contain yogurt and therefore have lovely, smooth sauces. A good accompaniment would be Chapatis (see page 180), or Fried Spicy Rice (see page 160) with peas.

Serves 6

INGREDIENTS

3 medium onions
3 medium potatoes
300 ml/^{1}/2 pint/1^1/4 cups oil
1 kg/2 lb 4 oz leg of lamb, cubed with
    or without bone
2 tsp garam masala
1^1/2 tsp fresh ginger root, finely
    chopped

1^1/2 tsp fresh garlic, crushed
1 tsp chilli powder
3 black peppercorns
3 green cardamoms
1 tsp black cumin seeds
2 cinnamon sticks
1 tsp paprika
1^1/2 tsp salt

150 ml/5 fl oz/^{2}/3 cup natural yogurt
600 ml/1 pint/2^1/2 cups water

TO GARNISH:
2 green chillies, chopped
fresh coriander (cilantro) leaves,
    chopped

1 Peel and slice the onions and set aside. Peel and cut each potato into 6 pieces.

2 Heat the oil in a saucepan and fry the sliced onions until golden brown. Remove the onions from the pan and set aside.

3 Add the meat to the saucepan with 5 ml/1 tsp of the garam masala and stir-fry for 5-7 minutes over a low heat.

4 Add the onions to the pan and remove from the heat.

5 Meanwhile in a small bowl, mix together the ginger, garlic, chilli powder, peppercorns, cardamoms, cumin seeds, cinnamon sticks, paprika and salt. Add the yogurt and mix well.

6 Return the pan to the heat and gradually add the spice and yogurt mixture to the meat

and onions and stir-fry for 7-10 minutes. Add the water, lower the heat and cook, covered, for about 40 minutes, stirring the mixture occasionally.

7 Add the potatoes to the pan and cook, covered, for a further 15 minutes, gently stirring the mixture occasionally. Garnish with green chillies and fresh coriander (cilantro) leaves, and serve at once.

Lean Lamb Cooked in Spinach

*I like to serve this nutritious combination of lamb and spinach with plain boiled
rice and Tomato Curry (see page 134).*

Serves 2–4

INGREDIENTS

300 ml/¹/₂ pint/1¹/₄ cups oil
2 medium onions, sliced
¹/₄ bunch fresh coriander (cilantro)
3 green chillies, chopped
1¹/₂ tsp fresh ginger root, finely
    chopped
1¹/₂ tsp fresh garlic, crushed
1 tsp chilli powder

¹/₂ tsp turmeric
450 g/1 lb lean lamb, with or
    without the bone
1 tsp salt
1 kg/2 lb 4 oz fresh spinach, trimmed,
    washed and chopped or 425g/
    15 oz can spinach
700 ml/1¹/₄ pints/3¹/₄ cups water

TO GARNISH:
fresh red chillies, finely chopped

1 Heat the oil in a saucepan and fry the onions until they turn a pale colour.

2 Add the fresh coriander (cilantro) and 2 of the chopped green chillies to the pan and stir-fry for 3-5 minutes.

3 Reduce the heat and add the ginger, garlic, chilli powder and turmeric to the mixture in the pan, stirring to mix.

4 Add the lamb to the pan and stir-fry for a further 5 minutes. Add the salt and the fresh or canned spinach and cook, stirring occasionally with a wooden spoon, for a further 3-5 minutes.

5 Add the water, stirring, and cook over a low heat, covered, for about 45 minutes. Remove the lid and check the meat. If it is not tender, turn the meat over, increase the heat and cook, uncovered, until the surplus water has been absorbed. Stir-fry the mixture for a further 5-7 minutes.

6 Transfer the lamb and spinach mixture to a serving dish and garnish with finely chopped red chillies. Serve hot.

Spicy Lamb Chops

This is an attractive way of serving lamb chops, especially if you garnish them with potato chips, tomatoes and lemon wedges. Serve these with any dhaal *and rice or chapatis (see page 180).*

Serves 4-6

INGREDIENTS

1 kg/2 lb 4 oz lamb chops
2 tsp fresh ginger root, finely
   chopped
2 tsp fresh garlic, crushed
1 tsp pepper
1 tsp garam masala

1 tsp black cumin seeds
1¹/₂ tsp salt
850 ml/1¹/₂ pints/3³/₄ cups water
2 medium eggs
300 ml/¹/₂ pint/1¹/₂ cups oil

TO GARNISH:
fried potato chips
tomatoes
lemon wedges

1 Using a sharp knife, trim away any excess fat from the lamb chops.

2 Mix the ginger, garlic, pepper, garam masala, cumin seeds and salt together and rub all over the chops.

3 Bring the water to a boil, add the chops and spice mixture and cook for about 45 minutes, stirring occasionally. Once the water has evaporated, remove from the heat and set aside to cool.

4 Using a fork, beat the eggs together in a large bowl.

5 Heat the oil in a large saucepan.

6 Dip each lamb chop into the beaten egg and then fry them in the oil for 3 minutes, turning once.

7 Transfer the chops to a large serving dish and garnish with fried potato chips, tomatoes and lemon wedges. Serve hot.

COOK'S TIP

Garam masala is a mixture of ground spices, not an individual spice. The usual combination includes cardamom, cinnamon, cloves, cumin, nutmeg and black peppercorns, but most Indian cooks have a personal recipe, often handed down for generations. You can buy prepared garam masala at large supermarkets or Asian grocery stores.

Stuffed Tomatoes

This is an impressive dinner-party dish – serve as a starter.
You will find large tomatoes are easier to fill.

Serves 4–6

INGREDIENTS

6 large, firm tomatoes
50 g/1³/4 oz/4 tbsp unsalted butter
1 medium onion, finely chopped
5 tbsp oil

1 tsp fresh ginger root, finely
  chopped
1 tsp fresh garlic, crushed
1 tsp pepper
1 tsp salt

1/2 tsp garam masala
450 g/1 lb minced lamb
1 green chilli
fresh coriander (cilantro) leaves

1 Preheat the oven to 180°C/
350°F/Gas Mark 4. Rinse
the tomatoes, cut off the tops
and scoop out the flesh.

2 Grease a heatproof dish with
50 g/1³/4 oz butter. Place the
tomatoes in the dish.

3 Heat the oil in a pan and fry
the onion until golden.

4 Lower the heat and add the
ginger, garlic, pepper, salt and
garam masala. Stir-fry the mixture
for 3-5 minutes.

5 Add the minced lamb to
the saucepan and fry for
10-15 minutes.

6 Add the green chilli and fresh
coriander (cilantro) leaves and
continue stir-frying the mixture
for 3-5 minutes.

7 Spoon the lamb mixture into
the tomatoes and replace the
tops. Cook the tomatoes in the
oven for 15-20 minutes.

8 Transfer the tomatoes to
serving plates and serve hot.

VARIATION

*You could use the same recipe to
stuff red or green (bell) peppers,
if you prefer.*

Cubed Lamb Kebabs (Kabobs)

I simply love these kebabs (kabobs) and remember going out in the evening in India just to have them sitting out in the open – they are barbecued (grilled) as you watch, to order.

Serves 6–8

INGREDIENTS

1 kg/2 lb 4 oz lean lamb, boned and cubed
1 tsp meat tenderizer
1¹/₂ tsp fresh ginger root, finely chopped
1¹/₂ tsp fresh garlic, crushed
1 tsp chilli powder

¹/₂ tsp turmeric
¹/₂ tsp salt
2 tbsp water
8 tomatoes, cut in half
8 small pickling onions
10 mushrooms

1 green (bell) pepper, cut into large pieces
1 red (bell) pepper, cut into large pieces
2 tbsp oil
2 lemons, cut into quarters, to garnish

1 Wash the meat and place it in a clean dish. Apply the tenderizer to the meat, using your hands. Set aside for about 3 hours at room temperature.

2 Mix together the ginger, garlic, chilli powder, turmeric and salt in a bowl. Add the water and mix to form a paste. Add the meat and mix until it is well coated with the spices.

3 Arrange the meat cubes on skewers, alternating with the tomatoes, pickling onions, mushrooms and (bell) peppers. Brush the meat and vegetables with the oil.

4 Grill (broil) the kebabs (kabobs) under a pre-heated grill (broiler) for 25-30 minutes or until the meat is cooked through. When cooked, remove the kebabs (kabobs) from the grill (broiler) and transfer to a serving plate. Arrange lemon wedges on the side and serve immediately with boiled rice and a Raita (see page 216).

COOK'S TIP

If using wooden skewers, soak them in cold water for 20 minutes before they are used to prevent them from burning during cooking.

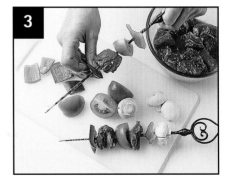

Cauliflower with Meat

I love vegetables cooked with meat, especially cauliflower and spinach, which have a lovely flavour cooked this way. I use only a few spices but I like to add a baghaar *(seasoned oil dressing) at the end.*

Serves 4

INGREDIENTS

1 medium cauliflower
2 green chillies
300 ml/^{1}/$_2$ pint/1^1/$_4$ cups oil
2 onions, sliced
450 g/1 lb cubed lamb
1^1/$_2$ tsp fresh ginger root, finely
   chopped

1^1/$_2$ tsp fresh garlic, crushed
1 tsp chilli powder
1 tsp salt
fresh coriander (cilantro) leaves,
   chopped
850 ml/1^1/$_2$ pints/3^3/$_4$ cups water
1 tbsp lemon juice

BAGHAAR:
150 ml/^{1}/$_4$ pint/^{2}/$_3$ cup oil
4 dried red chillies
1 tsp mixed mustard and
   onion seeds

1 Using a sharp knife, cut the cauliflower into small florets. Chop the green chillies finely.

2 Heat the oil in a large saucepan. Add the onions and fry until golden brown.

3 Reduce the heat and add the meat, stirring.

4 Add the ginger, garlic, chilli powder and salt. Stir-fry for about 5 minutes, stirring to mix.

5 Add 1 green chilli and half of the coriander (cilantro) leaves.

6 Stir in the water and cook, covered, over a low heat for about 30 minutes.

7 Add the cauliflower and simmer for a further 15-20 minutes or until the water has evaporated completely. Stir-fry the mixture for another 5 minutes. Remove the pan from the heat and sprinkle the lemon juice sparingly.

8 To make the *baghaar*, heat the remaining oil in a separate small saucepan. Add the dried red chillies and the mixed mustard and onion seeds and fry until they turn a darker colour, stirring occasionally. Remove the pan from the heat and pour the mixture over the cooked cauliflower.

9 Garnish with the remaining green chilli and fresh coriander (cilantro) leaves. Serve immediately.

Lamb & Lentils

In this recipe I use four different types of lentils and porridge oats. This takes some time to cook as you have to cook the lamb khorma *separately. However, the result is truly delicious!*

Serves 6

INGREDIENTS

100 g/3$^{1}/_{2}$ oz/$^{1}/_{2}$ cup *chana dhaal*
100 g/3$^{1}/_{2}$ oz/$^{1}/_{2}$ cup *masoor dhaal*
100 g/3$^{1}/_{2}$ oz/$^{1}/_{2}$ cup *moong dhaal*
100 g/3$^{1}/_{2}$ oz/$^{1}/_{2}$ cup *urid dhaal*
75 g/2$^{3}/_{4}$ oz/5 tbsp porridge oats

KHORMA:
1.5 kg/3 lb 5 oz lamb, cubed with
    bones
200 ml/7 fl oz/$^{3}/_{4}$ cup yogurt

2 tsp fresh ginger root, finely
    chopped
2 tsp fresh garlic, crushed
1 tbsp garam masala
2 tsp chilli powder
$^{1}/_{2}$ tsp turmeric
3 whole green cardamoms
2 cinnamon sticks
1 tsp black cumin seeds
2 tsp salt
450 ml/16 fl oz/2 cups oil

5 medium onions, sliced
700 ml/1$^{1}/_{4}$ pints/3$^{1}/_{4}$ cups water
2 green chillies
fresh coriander (cilantro) leaves

TO GARNISH:
6 green chillies, chopped
$^{1}/_{2}$ bunch fresh coriander (cilantro)
    leaves, chopped
2 pieces fresh ginger root, shredded
3 lemons, cut into wedges

1 Soak the *dhaals* and oats overnight. Boil in a pan of water until soft. Mash and set aside.

2 Place the lamb in a large bowl. Add the yogurt, spices and salt, mix and set aside.

3 Heat 300 ml/$^{1}/_{2}$ pint/1$^{1}/_{4}$ cups of the oil in a pan and fry 4 of the onions until golden. Add the meat and stir-fry for 7-10 minutes. Stir in the water, lower the heat and cook, covered, for 1 hour, stirring. If the meat is still not tender, add more water and cook for 15-20 minutes. Remove from the heat.

4 Add the *dhaals* to the meat, stir and mix. If the mixture is too thick, add 300 ml/$^{1}/_{2}$ pint/1$^{1}/_{4}$ cups water, stir and cook for 10-12 minutes. Add the chillies and the coriander (cilantro). Transfer to a serving dish and set aside.

5 Heat the remaining oil and fry the remaining onion until golden. Pour over the lamb and *lentils*. Garnish and serve.

Meatballs in Sauce

This is an old family recipe. The koftas *(meatballs) are easy
to make and also freeze beautifully.*

Serves 4

INGREDIENTS

450 g/1 lb minced lamb
1 tsp fresh ginger root, crushed
1 tsp fresh garlic, crushed
1 tsp garam masala
1^1/$_2$ tsp poppy seeds
1 tsp salt
^{1}/$_2$ tsp chilli powder
1 medium onion, finely chopped
1 green chilli, finely chopped
fresh coriander (cilantro) leaves

1 tbsp gram flour
150 ml/^{1}/$_4$ pint/^{2}/$_3$ cup oil

SAUCE:
2 tbsp oil
3 medium onions, finely chopped
2 small cinnamon sticks
2 large black cardamoms
1 tsp fresh ginger root, finely
  chopped

1 tsp fresh garlic, crushed
1 tsp salt
75 ml/3 fl oz/4^1/$_2$ tbsp natural yogurt
150 ml/^{1}/$_4$ pint/^{2}/$_3$ cup water

TO GARNISH:
fresh coriander (cilantro) leaves,
  finely chopped
1 green chilli, finely chopped

1 Place the lamb in a large mixing bowl.

2 Add the ginger, garlic, garam masala, poppy seeds, salt, chilli powder, onion, chilli, coriander (cilantro) and gram flour and mix well with a fork.

3 Make small meatballs out of the mixture with your hands and set aside.

4 To make the sauce, heat the oil and fry the onions until golden brown. Add the cinnamon sticks and cardamoms to the pan, lower the heat and stir-fry for a further 5 minutes. Add the ginger, garlic, salt, yogurt and water and stir to mix well.

5 Transfer to a serving bowl and garnish with chopped coriander (cilantro) and chillies.

6 Heat the oil and fry the meatballs, turning occasionally, for 8-10 minutes or until golden.

7 Transfer the meatballs to warm serving plates. Serve with the sauce and Chapatis (see page 180).

Spicy Lamb Curry in Sauce

This curry is especially good served with plain boiled rice and Onion Dhaal (see page 142). Tamarind is traditionally used for this recipe but I like to use lemon juice.

Serves 4

INGREDIENTS

2 tsp ground cumin
2 tsp ground coriander
2 tsp desiccated (shredded) coconut
1 tsp mixed mustard and onion seeds
2 tsp sesame seeds

1 tsp fresh ginger root, finely chopped
1 tsp fresh garlic, crushed
1 tsp chilli powder
1 tsp salt
450 g/1 lb lean lamb

450 ml/16 fl oz/2 cups oil
3 medium onions, sliced
850 ml/1¹/₂ pints/3³/₄ cups water
2 tbsp lemon juice
4 green chillies, split

1 Dry roast the ground cumin, ground coriander, desiccated (shredded) coconut, mixed mustard and onion seeds and the sesame seeds in a heavy frying pan (skillet), shaking the pan frequently to stop the spices from burning. Grind the roasted spices using a pestle and mortar.

2 In a large mixing bowl, blend together the roasted ground spices along with the ginger, garlic, chilli powder, salt and the cubed lamb and set aside.

3 In a separate pan, heat 300 ml/ ¹/₂ pint/1¹/₂ cups of the oil and fry the onions until golden brown.

4 Add the meat mixture to the onions and stir-fry for 5-7 minutes over a low heat. Add the water and simmer for 45 minutes, stirring occasionally. When the meat is cooked through, remove from the heat and sprinkle with the lemon juice.

5 In a separate saucepan, heat the remaining oil and add the

four split green chillies. Reduce the heat and cover with a lid. Remove the pan from the heat after about 30 seconds and set aside to cool.

6 Pour the chilli oil mixture over the meat curry and serve hot with Onion Dhaal (see page 142) and plain boiled rice.

Meat-Coated Eggs

These are ideal for taking on a picnic, because they are dry. In fact,
they are the Indian equivalent of the Scotch egg.

Serves 6

INGREDIENTS

450 g/1 lb lean minced lamb
1 small onion, finely chopped
1 green chilli, finely chopped
1 tsp fresh ginger root, finely
  chopped

1 tsp fresh garlic, crushed
1 tsp ground coriander
1 tsp garam masala
1 tsp salt

$1^1/_2$ tbsp gram flour
7 eggs, 6 of them hard-boiled (hard-
  cooked) and shelled, 1 beaten
oil, for deep-frying

1 Place the lamb, onion and the green chilli in a bowl and mix together. Transfer the mixture to a food processor and work until well ground. (Alternatively, grind by hand using a pestle and mortar).

2 Remove the mixture from the food processor and add the ginger, garlic, ground coriander, garam masala, salt, gram flour and the beaten egg. Combine the mixture together with your hands.

3 Divide the mixture into 6 equal portions. Roll each portion out to form a flat round,

about 5 mm/$^1/_4$ inch thick. Place a hard-boiled (hard-cooked) egg in the middle of each round and wrap the meat mixture around the egg to enclose it completely. When all 6 eggs have been covered, set aside in a cool place for 20-30 minutes.

4 Meanwhile, heat the oil in a *karahi* or deep frying pan (skillet). Gently drop the meat-coated eggs into the oil and fry for 2-4 minutes or until golden brown. Using a perforated spoon, remove the meat-coated eggs from the oil, transfer to kitchen paper and drain thoroughly. Serve hot.

VARIATION

If you wish to serve these Meat-Coated Eggs in a sauce, use the recipe for Meatballs in Sauce (see page 36).

Pork & Mushroom Curry

Vary the meat used here according to personal taste, using lean leg or shoulder of lamb or braising beef instead of pork. Omit the finishing touches (see step 5), if preferred.

Serves 4

INGREDIENTS

750 g/1 lb 10 oz leg or shoulder of pork
3 tbsp vegetable oil
2 onions, sliced
2 garlic cloves, crushed
2.5 cm/1 inch piece ginger root, chopped finely
2 fresh green chillies, seeded and chopped, or use 1-2 tsp minced

chilli (from a jar)
1^1/$_2$ tbsp medium curry paste
1 tsp ground coriander
175-250 g/6-9 oz mushrooms, sliced thickly
850 ml/1^1/$_2$ pints/3^1/$_2$ cups stock
3 tomatoes, chopped
^{1}/$_2$-1 tsp salt
60 g/2 oz creamed coconut, chopped

2 tbsp ground almonds

TO GARNISH:
2 tbsp vegetable oil
1 green or red (bell) pepper, seeded and cut into thin strips
6 spring onions (scallions), trimmed and sliced
1 tsp cumin seeds

1 Cut the pork into small bite-sized pieces. Heat the oil in a saucepan, add the pork and fry until sealed, stirring frequently. Remove the pork from the pan.

2 Add the onions, garlic, ginger, chillies, curry paste and coriander (cilantro) to the saucepan and cook gently for 2 minutes, Stir in the mushrooms, stock and tomatoes, and season with a little salt to taste.

3 Return the pork to the pan, then cover and simmer very gently for 1^1/$_4$-1^1/$_2$ hours or until the pork is tender.

4 Stir the creamed coconut and ground almonds into the curry, then cover the pan and cook gently for 3 minutes.

5 Meanwhile, make the garnish. Heat the oil in a frying pan (skillet), add the (bell) pepper strips and spring onion (scallion) slices and fry gently until glistening and tender-crisp. Stir in the cumin seeds and fry gently for 30 seconds. Spoon the mixture over the curry and serve at once.

COOK'S TIP

Creamed coconut is sold in compressed bars and gives a rich flavour and texture to dishes.

Beef Kebabs (Kabobs)

All my friends like this dish, which is always handy to have in the freezer. It is best served with Fried Spicy Rice (see page 160) and a dhaal *or a wet vegetable curry.*

Makes 10–12

INGREDIENTS

3 tbsp *chana dhaal*
450 g/1 lb lean beef, boned and cubed
1 tsp fresh ginger root, finely chopped
1 tsp fresh garlic, crushed
1 tsp chilli powder

1¹/₂ tsp salt
1¹/₂ tsp garam masala
3 green chillies
fresh coriander (cilantro) leaves
1 medium onion, chopped
300 ml/¹/₂ pint/1¹/₄ cups oil
850 ml/1¹/₂ pints/3¹/₂ cups water

2 tbsp natural yogurt
1 medium egg

TO GARNISH:
onion rings
green chillies

1 Rinse the *chana dhaal* twice, removing any stones or other impurities. Boil the *chana dhaal* in a pan of water until the water dries up and the *chana dhaal* has softened. Place in a food processor and mash to form a paste.

2 Mix the meat, ginger, garlic, chilli powder, salt and garam masala in a bowl. Add 2 of the green chillies, half of the fresh coriander (cilantro) leaves and the onion.

3 Heat 2 tbsp of the oil in a saucepan. Add the meat mixture to the pan. Add the water and cook, covered, over a low heat for 45-60 minutes. Once the meat is tender, evaporate any excess water by removing the lid and cooking for a further 10-15 minutes. Place the meat in a food processor and mash.

4 Place the yogurt, egg, mashed *chana dhaal* paste, the remaining green chilli and the coriander (cilantro) leaves in a bowl and mix together with your fingers. Break off small balls of the meat paste and make about 12 small, flat circular shapes with the palms of your hands.

5 Heat the remaining oil in a frying pan (skillet) and cook the rounds, in batches of 3, turning once.

6 Serve garnished with onion rings and green chillies.

Sliced Beef with Yogurt & Spices

There are many different ways of cooking this dish, but this is my particular favourite. However, for this recipe you need to roast the spices, as this helps give the dish a nice dark colour and a richer taste.

Serves 4

INGREDIENTS

450 g/1 lb lean beef slices, cut into
   2.5 cm/1-inch slices
5 tbsp yogurt
1 tsp fresh ginger root, finely
   chopped
1 tsp fresh garlic, crushed
1 tsp chilli powder
1 pinch turmeric

2 tsp garam masala
1 tsp salt
2 cardamoms
1 tsp black cumin seeds
50 g/1³/₄ oz/¹/₄ cup ground almonds
1 tbsp desiccated (shredded) coconut
1 tbsp poppy seeds
1 tbsp sesame seeds

300 ml/¹/₂ pint/1¹/₄ cups oil
2 medium onions, finely chopped
300 ml/¹/₂ pint/1¹/₄ cups water
2 green chillies, finely chopped
a few fresh coriander (cilantro)
   leaves, chopped
red chilli strips, to garnish

1 Place the beef in a large bowl, mix with the yogurt, ginger, garlic, chilli powder, turmeric, garam masala, salt, cardamoms and black cumin seeds and set aside until required.

2 Dry roast the ground almonds, desiccated (shredded) coconut, poppy seeds and sesame seeds in a heavy frying pan (skillet) until golden, shaking the pan to stop the spices from burning.

3 Work the spice mixture in a food processor until finely ground. (Add 1 tbsp of water to blend, if necessary.) Add the ground spice mixture to the meat mixture and combine.

4 Heat a little oil in a large saucepan and fry the onions until golden brown. Remove the onions from the pan. Stir-fry the meat in the remaining oil for about 5 minutes, then return the onions

to the pan and stir-fry for a further 5-7 minutes. Add the water and leave to simmer over a low heat, covered, for 25-30 minutes, stirring occasionally. Add the green chillies and coriander (cilantro) leaves, garnish and serve hot.

VARIATION

Substitute lamb for the beef in this recipe, if you prefer.

Beef Khorma with Almonds

This khorma, *a traditional northern Indian recipe,*
has a thick sauce and is quite simple to cook.

Serves 6

INGREDIENTS

300 ml/^{1}/$_2$ pint/1^1/$_4$ cups oil
3 medium onions, finely chopped
1 kg/2 lb 4 oz lean beef, cubed
1^1/$_2$ tsp garam masala
1^1/$_2$ tsp ground coriander
1^1/$_2$ tsp fresh ginger root, finely
   chopped

1^1/$_2$ tsp fresh garlic, crushed
1 tsp salt
150 ml/5 fl oz/^{2}/$_3$ cup natural yogurt
2 cloves
3 green cardamoms
4 black peppercorns
600 ml/1 pint/2^1/$_2$ cups water

TO GARNISH:
6 almonds, soaked, peeled and
   chopped
2 green chillies, chopped
a few fresh coriander (cilantro) leaves

1 Heat the oil in a saucepan. Add the onions and stir-fry until golden brown. Remove half of the onions from the pan, set aside and reserve.

2 Add the meat to the remaining onions in the pan and stir-fry for about 5 minutes. Remove the pan from the heat.

3 Mix the garam masala, ground coriander, ginger, garlic, salt and yogurt in a bowl.

Gradually add the meat to the yogurt and spice mixture and mix to coat the meat on all sides. Place in the saucepan, return to the heat, and stir-fry for 5-7 minutes, or until the mixture is nearly brown in colour.

4 Add the cloves, green cardamoms and black peppercorns. Add the water, lower the heat, cover and leave to simmer for about 45-60 minutes. If the water has completely

evaporated but the meat is still not tender enough, add another 300 ml/^{1}/$_2$ pint/1^1/$_2$ cups water and cook for a further 10-15 minutes, stirring occasionally.

5 Just before serving, garnish with the reserved onions, chopped almonds, green chillies and the fresh coriander (cilantro) leaves. Serve with Chapatis (see page 180).

Beef Cooked in Whole Spices

*This is a delicious way of cooking beef. The fragrant whole
spices perfectly complement the meat.*

Serves 4

INGREDIENTS

300 ml/^{1}/$_2$ pint/1^1/$_4$ cups oil
3 medium onions, chopped finely
2.5 cm/1 inch ginger root, shredded
4 cloves garlic, shredded
2 cinnamon sticks

3 whole green cardamoms
3 whole cloves
4 whole black peppercorns
6 dried red chillies
150 ml/5 fl oz/^{2}/$_3$ cup yogurt

450 g/1 lb beef, with or without
   bone, cut into cubes
3 green chillies, chopped
600 ml/1 pint/2^1/$_2$ cups water
fresh coriander (cilantro) leaves

1 Heat the oil in a frying pan
(skillet) and fry the onion,
stirring, until golden brown.

2 Reduce the heat and add the
ginger, garlic, cinnamon sticks,
green cardamoms, cloves, black
peppercorns and red chillies to the
pan and stir-fry for 5 minutes.

3 In a bowl, whip the yogurt
with a fork. Add the yogurt to
the onions and stir to combine.

4 Add the meat and 2 of the
green chillies to the frying
pan (skillet) and stir-fry the
mixture for 5-7 minutes.

5 Gradually add the water to the
pan, stirring well. Cover the
pan and cook the beef and spice
mixture for 1 hour, stirring and
adding more water if necessary.

6 When thoroughly cooked
through, remove the pan
from the heat and transfer the beef
and spice mixture to a serving
dish. Garnish with the remaining
chopped green chilli and the fresh
coriander (cilantro) leaves.

VARIATION

*Substitute lamb for the beef in this
recipe, if you prefer.*

Fried Kidneys

Fried lamb kidneys are a popular dish for a late breakfast or brunch,
served with Paratas (see page 174) and a fried egg.

Serves 4

INGREDIENTS

450 g/1 lb lamb's kidneys
2 tsp turmeric
2¹/₂ tsp salt
150 ml/¹/₄ pint/²/₃ cup water

1 green (bell) pepper, sliced
1 tsp fresh ginger root, finely
  chopped
1 tsp fresh garlic, crushed

1 tsp chilli powder
3 tbsp oil
1 small onion, finely chopped
coriander (cilantro) leaves, to garnish

1 Using a sharp knife, remove the very fine skin surrounding each kidney. Cut each kidney into 4-6 pieces.

2 Place the kidney pieces in a bowl with the turmeric and 2 teaspoons of salt. Pour in the water, mix to combine and leave to marinate for about 1 hour. Drain the kidneys thoroughly, then rinse them under cold running water until the water runs clear.

3 Place the kidneys in a small saucepan together with the green (bell) pepper. Pour in

enough water to cover and cook over a medium heat, leaving the lid of the pan slightly ajar so that the steam can escape, until all of the water has evaporated.

4 Add the ginger, garlic, chilli powder and remaining salt to the kidney mixture and blend until well combined.

5 Add the oil, onion and the coriander (cilantro) to the pan, and stir-fry for 7-10 minutes.

6 Transfer the kidneys to a serving plate and serve hot.

COOK'S TIP

Many people are resistant to the idea of cooking or eating kidneys because they often have rather a strong smell – even when cooked. However, if you wash and soak them in water, you can largely avoid this problem.

Chicken Tikka

*For this very popular dish, small pieces of chicken are marinated
for a minimum of 3 hours in yogurt and spices.*

Serves 6

INGREDIENTS

1 tsp fresh ginger root, finely
   chopped
1 tsp fresh garlic, crushed
$\frac{1}{2}$ tsp ground coriander
$\frac{1}{2}$ tsp ground cumin
1 tsp chilli powder
3 tbsp yogurt

1 tsp salt
2 tbsp lemon juice
a few drops of red food colouring
   (optional)
1 tbsp tomato purée (paste)
1.5 kg/3 lb 5 oz chicken breast
1 onion, sliced

3 tbsp oil

TO GARNISH:
6 lettuce leaves
1 lemon, cut into wedges

1 Blend together the ginger, garlic, ground coriander, ground cumin and chilli powder in a large mixing bowl.

2 Add the yogurt, salt, lemon juice, red food colouring (if using) and the tomato purée (paste) to the spice mixture.

3 Using a sharp knife, cut the chicken into pieces. Add the chicken to the spice mixture and toss to coat well. Leave to marinate for at least 3 hours, preferably overnight.

4 Arrange the onion in the bottom of a heatproof dish. Carefully drizzle half of the oil over the onions.

5 Arrange the marinated chicken pieces on top of the onions and cook under a pre-heated grill (broiler), turning once and basting with the remaining oil, for 25-30 minutes.

6 Serve the chicken tikka on a bed of lettuce and garnish with the lemon wedges.

COOK'S TIP

*Chicken Tikka can be served with
Naan Breads (see page 178), Raita
(see page 216) and Mango
Chutney (see page 218)
or as a starter.*

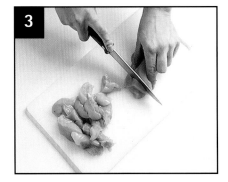

Chicken Kebabs (Kabobs)

These kebabs (kabobs) are a deliciously different way of serving chicken.
Serve with any dhaal *and Chapatis (see page 180).*

Serves 6-8

INGREDIENTS

1.5 kg/3 lb 5 oz chicken, boned
$^1/_2$ tsp ground cumin
4 cardamom seeds, crushed
$^1/_2$ tsp ground cinnamon
1 tsp salt
1 tsp fresh ginger root, finely
   chopped

1 tsp fresh garlic, crushed
$^1/_2$ tsp ground allspice
$^1/_2$ tsp pepper
300 ml/$^1/_2$ pint/1$^1/_4$ cups water
2 tbsp yogurt
2 green chillies

1 small onion
fresh coriander (cilantro) leaves
1 medium egg, beaten
300 ml/$^1/_2$ pint/1$^1/_4$ cups oil
green salad leaves and lemon
   wedges, to garnish

1 Place the boned chicken in a large saucepan. Add the ground cumin, cardamom seeds, ground cinnamon, salt, ginger, garlic, ground allspice and pepper and pour in the water. Bring the mixture to the boil until all of the water has been absorbed.

2 Put the mixture in a food processor and grind to form a smooth paste. Transfer the paste to a mixing bowl. Add the yogurt and blend together until well combined.

3 Place the green chillies, onion and coriander (cilantro) leaves in the food processor and grind finely. Add to the chicken mixture and mix well. Add the beaten egg and mix to combine.

4 Break off 12-15 portions from the mixture and make small, flat round shapes in the palm of your hand.

5 Heat the oil in a saucepan and fry the kebabs (kabobs) gently, in batches, over a low heat, turning once. Drain thoroughly on kitchen paper and serve hot.

COOK'S TIP

Indian kebab (kabob) dishes are not necessarily cooked on a skewer; they can also be served in a dish and are always dry dishes with no sauce.

Chicken & Onions

This dish represents one of the rare occasions when we do not use yogurt to cook chicken.
It has a lovely flavour and is perfect served with Pulao Rice (see page 158). It also freezes very well.

Serves 4

INGREDIENTS

300 ml/^{1}/$_2$ pint/1^1/$_4$ cups oil
4 medium onions, finely chopped
1^1/$_2$ tsp fresh ginger root, finely
   chopped
1^1/$_2$ tsp garam masala
1^1/$_2$ tsp fresh garlic, crushed

1 tsp chilli powder
1 tsp ground coriander
3 whole cardamoms
3 peppercorns
3 tbsp tomato purée (paste)
8 chicken thighs, skinned

300 ml/^{1}/$_2$ pint/1^1/$_4$ cups water
2 tbsp lemon juice
1 green chilli
fresh coriander (cilantro) leaves
green chilli strips, to garnish

1 Heat the oil in a large frying pan (skillet). Add the onion and fry, stirring occasionally, until golden brown.

2 Reduce the heat and add the ginger, garam masala, garlic, chilli powder, ground coriander, whole cardamoms and the peppercorns, stirring to mix.

3 Add the tomato purée (paste) to the mixture in the frying pan (skillet) and stir-fry for 5-7 minutes.

4 Add the chicken thighs to the pan and toss to coat with the spice mixture.

5 Pour the water into the saucepan, cover and leave to simmer for 20-25 minutes.

6 Add the lemon juice, green chilli and coriander (cilantro) to the mixture, and combine.

7 Transfer the chicken and onions to serving plates, garnish and serve hot.

COOK'S TIP

A dish of meat cooked with plenty of onions is called a Do Pyaza. *This curry definitely improves if made in advance and then reheated before serving. This develops the flavours and makes them deeper.*

Chicken Drumsticks Deep-Fried with Herbs & Spices

One of my favourite dinner-party dishes, this is very attractive to look at. It should ideally be cooked and served from a karahi, *but if you do not have one a deep, heavy frying-pan (skillet) will do.*

Serves 4

INGREDIENTS

8 chicken drumsticks
1¹/₂ tsp fresh ginger root, finely chopped
1¹/₂ tsp fresh garlic, crushed
1 tsp salt
2 medium onions, chopped

¹/₂ large bunch fresh coriander (cilantro) leaves
4-6 green chillies
600 ml/1 pint/2¹/₂ cups oil
4 firm tomatoes, cut into wedges

2 large green (bell) peppers, roughly chopped

1 Make 2-3 slashes in each piece of chicken. Rub the ginger, garlic and salt over the chicken pieces and set aside.

2 Place half of the onions, the coriander (cilantro) leaves and green chillies in a pestle and mortar and grind to a paste. Rub the paste over the chicken pieces.

3 Heat the oil in a *karahi* or large frying pan (skillet). Add the remaining onions and fry until golden brown. Remove the onions from the pan with a perforated spoon and set aside.

4 Reduce the heat to medium hot and fry the chicken pieces, in batches of about 2 at a time, until cooked through (about 5-7 minutes per piece).

5 When all of the chicken pieces are cooked through, remove them from the pan, keep warm and set aside.

6 Add the tomatoes and the (bell) peppers to the pan and half-cook them until they are softened but still have 'bite'.

7 Transfer the tomatoes and (bell) peppers to a serving plate and arrange the chicken on top. Garnish with the reserved fried onions.

Chicken Khorma

Chicken khorma *is one of the most popular curries,
and this one is perfect for a dinner party.*

Serves 4–6

INGREDIENTS

1¹/₂ tsp fresh ginger root, finely
   chopped
1¹/₂ tsp fresh garlic, crushed
2 tsp garam masala
1 tsp chilli powder
1 tsp salt
1 tsp black cumin seeds

3 green cardamoms, with husks
   removed and seeds crushed
1 tsp ground coriander
1 tsp ground almonds
150 ml/5 fl oz/²/₃ cup natural yogurt
8 whole chicken breasts, skinned
300 ml/¹/₂ pint/1¹/₄ cups oil

2 medium onions, sliced
150 ml/¹/₄ pint/²/₃ cup water
fresh coriander (cilantro) leaves
green chillies, chopped
boiled rice, to serve

1 Mix the ginger, garlic, garam masala, chilli powder, salt, black cumin seeds, green cardamoms, ground coriander and almonds with the yogurt.

2 Spoon the yogurt and spice mixture over the chicken breasts and set aside to marinate.

3 Heat the oil in a large frying pan (skillet). Add the onions to the pan and fry until a golden brown colour.

4 Add the chicken breasts to the pan, stir-frying for 5–7 minutes.

5 Add the water, cover and leave to simmer for 20–25 minutes.

6 Add the coriander (cilantro) and green chillies and cook for a further 10 minutes, stirring gently from time to time.

7 Transfer to a serving plate and serve with boiled rice.

VARIATION

Chicken portions may be used instead of breasts, if preferred, and should be cooked for 10 minutes longer in step 5.

Buttered Chicken

A simple and mouth-watering dish with a lovely thick sauce,
this makes an impressive centrepiece for a dinner party.

Serves 4-6

INGREDIENTS

100 g/3$^{1}/_{2}$ oz/8 tbsp unsalted butter
1 tbsp oil
2 medium onions, finely chopped
1 tsp fresh ginger root, finely
   chopped
2 tsp garam masala
2 tsp ground coriander
1 tsp chilli powder

1 tsp black cumin seeds
1 tsp fresh garlic, crushed
1 tsp salt
3 whole green cardamoms
3 whole black peppercorns
150 ml/5 fl oz/$^{2}/_{3}$ cup natural yogurt
2 tbsp tomato purée (paste)
8 chicken pieces, skinned

150 ml/$^{1}/_{4}$ pint/$^{2}/_{3}$ cup water
2 whole bay leaves
150 ml/5 fl oz/$^{2}/_{3}$ cup single (light)
   cream

TO GARNISH:
fresh coriander (cilantro) leaves
2 green chillies, chopped

1 Heat the butter and oil in a large frying pan (skillet). Add the onions and fry until golden brown, stirring. Reduce the heat.

2 Crush the fresh ginger and place in a bowl. Add the garam masala, ground coriander, ginger, chilli powder, black cumin seeds, garlic, salt, cardamoms and black peppercorns and blend. Add the yogurt and tomato purée (paste) and stir to combine.

3 Add the chicken pieces to the yogurt and spice mixture and mix to coat well.

4 Add the chicken to the onions in the pan and stir-fry vigorously, making semi-circular movements, for 5-7 minutes.

5 Add the water and the bay leaves to the mixture in the pan and leave to simmer for 30 minutes, stirring occasionally.

6 Add the cream and cook for a further 10-15 minutes.

7 Garnish with fresh coriander (cilantro) leaves and chillies and serve hot.

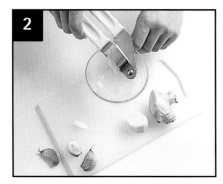

Tandoori-Style Chicken

In India, tandoori chicken is traditionally cooked in a tandoor (clay) oven. Alternatively, I pre-heat the grill (broiler) to a very high temperature then lower it to medium to cook this dish.

Serves 4

INGREDIENTS

8 chicken drumsticks, skinned
150 ml/5 fl oz/²/₃ cup natural yogurt
1¹/₂ tsp fresh ginger root, finely
   chopped
1¹/₂ tsp fresh garlic, crushed
1 tsp chilli powder
2 tsp ground cumin

2 tsp ground coriander
1 tsp salt
¹/₂ tsp red food colouring
1 tbsp tamarind paste
150 ml/¹/₄ pint/²/₃ cup water
150 ml/¹/₄ pint/²/₃ cup oil
lettuce leaves, to serve

TO GARNISH:
onion rings
sliced tomatoes
lemon wedges

1 Make 2-3 slashes in each piece of chicken.

2 Place the yogurt in a bowl. Add the ginger, garlic, chilli powder, ground cumin, ground coriander, salt and red food colouring and blend together until well combined.

3 Add the chicken to the yogurt and spice mixture and mix to coat well. Leave the chicken to marinate in the refrigerator for a minimum of 3 hours.

4 In a separate bowl, mix the tamarind paste with the water and fold into the yogurt and spice mixture. Toss the chicken pieces in this mixture and set aside to marinate for a further 3 hours.

5 Transfer the chicken pieces to a heatproof dish and brush the chicken with oil. Cook the chicken under a pre-heated medium-hot grill (broiler) for 30-35 minutes, turning the chicken pieces occasionally and basting with the remaining oil.

6 Arrange the chicken on a bed of lettuce and garnish with onion rings, sliced tomatoes and lemon wedges.

COOK'S TIP

Serve the succulent chicken pieces on a bed of lettuce, and garnished with a few onion rings, sliced tomatoes and lemon wedges. Naan Bread (see page 178) and Mint Raita (see page 216) complement the dish perfectly.

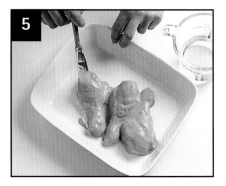

Spicy Roast Chicken

This chicken dish, ideal for dinner parties, is cooked in the oven – which is very rare in Indian cooking. The chicken can be boned, if desired.

Serves 4

INGREDIENTS

50 g/1³/₄ oz/¹/₄ cup ground almonds
50 g/1³/₄ oz/¹/₃ cup desiccated
   (shredded) coconut
150 ml/¹/₄ pint/²/₃ cup oil
1 medium onion, finely chopped
1 tsp fresh ginger root, chopped

1 tsp fresh garlic, crushed
1 tsp chilli powder
1¹/₂ tsp garam masala
1 tsp salt
150 ml/5 fl oz/²/₃ cup yogurt
4 chicken quarters, skinned

green salad leaves, to serve

TO GARNISH:
fresh coriander (cilantro) leaves
1 lemon, cut into wedges

1 In a heavy-based saucepan, dry roast the ground almonds and coconut and set aside.

2 Heat the oil in a frying pan (skillet) and fry the onion, stirring, until golden brown.

3 Place the ginger, garlic, chilli powder, garam masala and salt in a bowl and mix with the yogurt. Add the almonds and coconut and mix well.

4 Add the onions to the spice mixture, blend and set aside.

5 Arrange the chicken quarters in the bottom of a heatproof dish. Spoon the spice mixture over the chicken sparingly.

6 Cook in a pre-heated oven, 160°C/425°F/Gas Mark 3, for 35-45 minutes. Check that the chicken is cooked thoroughly by piercing the thickest part of the meat with a sharp knife or a fine skewer – the juices will run clear when the chicken is cooked through. Garnish with the coriander (cilantro) and lemon wedges and serve with a salad.

COOK'S TIP

If you want a more spicy dish, add more chilli powder and garam masala.

Chicken Jalfrezi

This is a quick and tasty way to use leftover roast chicken. The sauce can also be used for any cooked poultry, lamb or beef.

Serves 4

INGREDIENTS

1 tsp mustard oil
3 tbsp vegetable oil
1 large onion, chopped finely
3 garlic cloves, crushed
1 tbsp tomato purée (paste)
2 tomatoes, peeled and chopped
1 tsp ground turmeric

$^{1}/_{2}$ tsp cumin seeds, ground
$^{1}/_{2}$ tsp coriander seeds, ground
$^{1}/_{2}$ tsp chilli powder
$^{1}/_{2}$ tsp garam masala
1 tsp red wine vinegar
1 small red (bell) pepper, chopped

125 g/4 oz/1 cup frozen broad (fava) beans
500 g/1 lb cooked chicken breasts, cut into bite-sized pieces
salt
fresh coriander (cilantro) sprigs, to garnish

1 Heat the mustard oil in a large, frying pan (skillet) set over a high heat for about 1 minute until it begins to smoke. Add the vegetable oil, reduce the heat and then add the onion and the garlic. Fry the garlic and onion until they are golden.

2 Add the tomato purée (paste), chopped tomatoes, ground turmeric, cumin and coriander seeds, chilli powder, garam masala and red wine vinegar to the frying pan (skillet). Stir the mixture until fragrant.

3 Add the red (bell) pepper and broad (fava) beans and stir for 2 minutes until the (bell) pepper is softened. Stir in the chicken, and salt to taste. Leave to simmer gently for 6-8 minutes until the chicken is heated through and the beans are tender.

4 Serve garnished with coriander (cilantro) leaves.

COOK'S TIP

This dish is an ideal way of making use of leftover poultry – turkey, duck or quail. Any variety of beans works well, but vegetables are just as useful, especially root vegetables, courgettes (zucchini), potatoes or broccoli. Leafy vegetables will not be so successful.

Fried Fish in Gram Flour

*Very simple to make, this fried fish dish goes very well
with Tomato Curry (see page 134) and Fried Spicy Rice (see page 160).*

Serves 4–6

INGREDIENTS

100 g/3^1/$_2$ oz/^{3}/$_4$ cup gram flour
1 tsp fresh ginger root, finely
   chopped
1 tsp fresh garlic, crushed
2 tsp chilli powder
1 tsp salt

^{1}/$_2$ tsp turmeric
2 fresh green chillies, chopped
fresh coriander (cilantro) leaves,
   chopped
300 ml/^{1}/$_2$ pint/1^1/$_4$ cups water
1 kg/2 lb 4 oz cod

300 ml/^{1}/$_2$ pint/1^1/$_4$ cups oil
cooked rice, to serve

TO GARNISH:
2 lemons, cut into wedges
6 green chillies, slit down the middle

1 Place the gram flour in a large mixing bowl. Add the ginger, garlic, chilli powder, salt and turmeric and mix to blend well.

2 Add the green chillies and the coriander (cilantro) leaves to the spiced mixture and stir to mix well.

3 Pour in the water and stir to form a semi-thick batter. Set aside until required.

4 Using a sharp knife, cut the cod into about 8 pieces.

5 Carefully dip the pieces of cod into the batter, coating the cod all over. Shake off any excess batter.

6 Heat the oil in a heavy-based frying-pan (skillet). Add the battered cod and fry, in batches, over a medium heat, turning once, until cooked through and golden.

7 Transfer the battered cod to a serving dish and garnish with the lemon wedges and green chillies. Serve the cod with cooked rice.

COOK'S TIP

Gram flour or chana dhaal flour (lentil flour) is used to make Pakoras (see page 174) and is also used to bind kebabs (kabobs) and other items. A combination of gram flour and ordinary wholemeal flour makes a delicious Indian bread (see page 176).

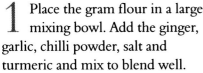

Bengali-Style Fish

Fresh fish is eaten a great deal in Bengal (Bangladesh), and this dish is made with mustard oil which gives the fish a good flavour.

Serves 4-6

INGREDIENTS

1 tsp turmeric
1 tsp salt
1 kg/2 lb 4 oz cod fillet, skinned and
   cut into pieces
6 tbsp corn oil

4 green chillies
1 tsp fresh ginger root, finely
   chopped
1 tsp fresh garlic, crushed
2 medium onions, finely chopped

2 tomatoes, finely chopped
6 tbsp mustard oil
450 ml/$^3/_4$ pint/2 cups water
fresh coriander (cilantro) leaves,
   chopped, to garnish

1 Mix together the turmeric and salt in a small bowl.

2 Spoon the turmeric and salt mixture over the fish pieces.

3 Heat the oil in a frying-pan (skillet). Add the fish to the pan and fry until pale yellow. Remove the fish with a perforated spoon and set aside.

4 Place the green chillies, ginger, garlic, onions, tomatoes and mustard oil in a pestle and mortar and grind to form a paste. Alternatively, work the ingredients in a food processor.

5 Transfer the spice paste to a saucepan and dry-fry until golden brown.

6 Remove the pan from the heat and gently place the fish pieces into the paste without breaking the fish up.

7 Return the pan to the heat, add the water and cook the fish, uncovered, over a medium heat for 15-20 minutes.

8 Serve garnished with chopped coriander (cilantro).

COOK'S TIP

In the hot and humid eastern plains that surround Bengal, the mustard plant flourishes, providing oil for cooking and spicy seeds for flavouring. Fish and seafood appear in many meals, often flavoured with mustard oil.

Prawns (Shrimp) with (Bell) Peppers

This is a colourful and impressive side dish for a dinner party. As there are not many spices in this recipe I like to use a lot of fresh coriander (cilantro) in it.

Serves 4

INGREDIENTS

450 g/1 lb frozen prawns (shrimp)
¹/₂ bunch fresh coriander (cilantro) leaves

1 tsp fresh garlic, crushed
1 tsp salt
1 medium green (bell) pepper, sliced

1 medium red (bell) pepper
75 g/2³/₄ oz/5¹/₂ tbsp unsalted butter

1 Defrost the prawns (shrimp) and rinse under cold running water twice. Drain the prawns (shrimp) thoroughly and place in a large mixing bowl.

2 Using a sharp knife, finely chop the bunch of fresh coriander (cilantro).

3 Add the garlic, salt and fresh coriander (cilantro) leaves to the prawns (shrimp) and set aside until required.

4 Deseed the (bell) peppers and cut into thin slices, using a sharp knife.

5 Melt the butter in a large frying pan (skillet). Add the prawns (shrimp) to the pan and stir-fry, stirring and tossing the prawns (shrimp) gently, for 10-12 minutes.

6 Add the (bell) peppers to the pan and fry for a further 3-5 minutes, stirring occasionally.

7 Transfer the prawns (shrimp) and (bell) pepper to a serving dish and serve hot.

VARIATION
You could use large tiger prawns (shrimp) in this dish, if you prefer.

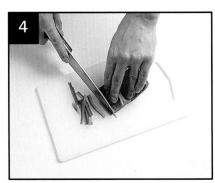

Prawns (Shrimp) with Spinach

*This is an attractive dish to serve as an accompaniment,
especially at parties, and will also freeze well.*

Serves 4–6

INGREDIENTS

225 g/8 oz frozen prawns (shrimp)
350 g/12 oz canned spinach purée or
 frozen spinach, thawed and
 chopped

2 tomatoes
150 ml/$^1/_4$ pint/$^2/_3$ cup oil
$^1/_2$ tsp mustard seeds
$^1/_2$ tsp onion seeds

1 tsp fresh ginger root, finely
 chopped
1 tsp fresh garlic, crushed
1 tsp chilli powder
1 tsp salt

1 Place the prawns (shrimp) in a bowl of cold water and set aside to defrost thoroughly.

2 Drain the can of spinach purée, if using.

3 Using a sharp knife, cut the tomatoes into slices.

4 Heat the oil in a large frying pan (skillet). Add the mustard and onion seeds to the pan.

5 Reduce the heat and add the tomatoes, spinach, ginger, garlic, chilli powder and salt to the pan and stir-fry for about 5-7 minutes.

6 Drain the prawns (shrimp) thoroughly.

7 Add the prawns (shrimp) to the spinach mixture in the pan. Gently stir the prawn (shrimp) and spinach mixture until well combined, cover and leave to simmer over a low heat for about 7-10 minutes.

8 Transfer the prawns (shrimp) and spinach to a serving dish and serve hot.

COOK'S TIP

If using frozen spinach, it should be thawed and squeezed dry before using. You could use fresh spinach, if you prefer.

Tandoori-Style Prawns (Shrimp)

These mouth-watering prawns (shrimp) can be served as a starter arranged on a bed of lettuce with a lemon wedge, or as an attractive side dish for almost any meal.

Serves 4

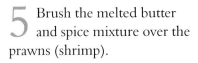

INGREDIENTS

10-12 king prawns (shrimp)
100 g/3¹/₂ oz/8 tbsp unsalted butter
1 tsp fresh ginger root, finely
  chopped
1 tsp fresh garlic, crushed
1 tsp chilli powder

¹/₂ tsp salt
1 tsp ground coriander
1 tsp ground cumin
fresh coriander (cilantro) leaves,
  finely chopped
a few drops of red food colouring

TO GARNISH:
8 lettuce leaves
1-2 green chillies, finely chopped
1 lemon, cut into wedges

1 Carefully remove the shells from the prawns (shrimp).

2 Transfer the shelled prawns (shrimp) to a heatproof dish.

3 Melt the butter in a large saucepan.

4 Add the ginger, garlic, chilli powder, salt, ground coriander, ground cumin, fresh coriander (cilantro) leaves and the red food colouring to the butter and mix together until well combined.

5 Brush the melted butter and spice mixture over the prawns (shrimp).

6 Cook the prawns (shrimp), under a very hot pre-heated grill (broiler), for 10-12 minutes, turning once.

7 Serve the prawns (shrimp) on a bed of lettuce and garnish with finely chopped green chillies and lemon wedges.

COOK'S TIP

Though not essential, it is best to shell the prawns (shrimp) before cooking them as some people find it a bit awkward to shell them at the table.

Dried Prawns (Shrimp)

This is a more economical way of cooking prawns (shrimp). You can buy the dried prawns (shrimp) in packets from most Indian and Pakistani grocers.

Serves 4

INGREDIENTS

200 g/7 oz dried prawns (shrimp)
2 medium onions, sliced
3 green chillies, finely chopped
fresh coriander (cilantro) leaves, finely chopped

300 ml/^{1}/$_2$ pint/1^1/$_4$ cups oil
1^1/$_2$ tsp fresh ginger root, finely chopped
1^1/$_2$ tsp fresh garlic, crushed
pinch of turmeric

1 tsp salt
1 tsp chilli powder, plus extra to garnish
2 tbsp lemon juice

1 Soak the prawns (shrimp) in a bowl of cold water for about 2 hours. Drain the prawns (shrimp) thoroughly and rinse under cold running water twice. Drain the prawns (shrimp) again thoroughly.

2 Heat 150 ml/^{1}/$_4$ pint/^{2}/$_3$ cup of the oil in a large saucepan.

3 Add the onions, 2 of the green chillies and half of the fresh coriander (cilantro) leaves to the pan and stir-fry until the onions are golden brown.

4 Add the ginger, garlic, turmeric, salt and chilli powder to the pan and stir-fry for a further 2 minutes over a low heat. Set aside until required.

5 Heat the remaining oil in a separate saucepan. Add the prawns (shrimp) and fry, stirring occasionally, until the prawns (shrimp) are crisp.

6 Add the fried prawns (shrimp) to the onions and blend together. Return the prawn (shrimp) and onion mixture to the heat, sprinkle with the lemon juice and stir-fry for 3-5 minutes.

7 Transfer the prawns (shrimp) to a serving dish, garnish with a pinch of chilli powder and serve with Chapatis (see page 180).

VARIATION

You could use 450 g/1 lb fresh prawns (shrimp) instead of the dried prawns (shrimp), if you prefer.

Prawns (Shrimp) with Tomatoes

Quick and easy to prepare, this dish is also extremely good to eat. Use the larger tiger prawns (shrimp) for special occasions, if you prefer.

Serves 4–6

INGREDIENTS

3 medium onions
1 green (bell) pepper
1 tsp fresh ginger root, finely
   chopped

1 tsp fresh garlic, crushed
1 tsp salt
1 tsp chilli powder
2 tbsp lemon juice

350 g/12 oz frozen prawns (shrimp)
3 tbsp oil
400 g/14 oz can tomatoes
fresh coriander (cilantro) leaves,
   to decorate

1 Using a sharp knife, slice the onions and the green (bell) pepper.

2 Place the ginger, garlic, salt and chilli powder in a small bowl and mix to combine. Add the lemon juice and mix to form a paste.

3 Place the prawns (shrimp) in a bowl of cold water and set aside to defrost. Drain thoroughly.

4 Heat the oil in a medium-sized saucepan. Add the onions and fry until golden brown.

5 Add the spice paste to the onions, reduce the heat to low and cook, stirring and mixing well, for about 3 minutes.

6 Add the tomatoes, tomato juice and the green (bell) pepper, and cook for 5-7 minutes, stirring occasionally.

7 Add the prawns (shrimp) to the pan and cook for 10 minutes, stirring occasionally. Garnish with fresh coriander (cilantro) leaves and serve hot with plain boiled rice and a crisp green salad.

COOK'S TIP

Fresh ginger root looks rather like a knobbly potato. The skin should be peeled, then the flesh either grated, finely chopped or sliced. Ginger is also available ground: this can be used as a substitute for fresh root ginger, but the fresh root is far superior.

Vegetables

A great many people in India are
vegetarians – possibly the majority. The reasons
for this are mainly religious, so over the years Indians
have used their imaginations to create a vast majority of
different vegetarian dishes. Spinach, tomatoes, potatoes,
green beans and cauliflower are all commonly used in
Indian cooking, but some popular Indian vegetables,
including aubergines (eggplants), okra (lady's fingers)
and mooli (white radish), are less familiar in the West
despite the fact that they are now widely available.
In this chapter, I have included some simple but
delicious vegetarian dishes using these vegetables –
some in a sauce, some dry – that will help you
to familirize yourself with them.

In strict vegetarian households, neither fish
nor even eggs are included in the diet, which
means it lacks protein (and certain vitamins). That
is why it is important to serve a dhaal (lentils) as part
of a vegetarian meal – all lentils are packed with
protein. A Raita (see page 216) makes an excellent
accompaniment to any vegetarian meal, and for
carbohydrate I think the best choice is plain boiled rice
or Pooris (see page 184).

Green Bean & Potato Curry

You can use fresh or canned green beans for this semi-dry vegetable curry. I would recommend you serve an Oil-dressed dhaal (see page 144) with this, for a good contrast of flavours and colours.

Serves 4

INGREDIENTS

300 ml/^{1}/2 pint/1^1/4 cups oil
1 tsp white cumin seeds
1 tsp mustard and onion seeds
4 dried red chillies
3 fresh tomatoes, sliced

1 tsp salt
1 tsp fresh ginger root, finely chopped
1 tsp fresh garlic, crushed
1 tsp chilli powder

200 g/7 oz green cut beans
2 medium potatoes, peeled and diced
300 ml/^{1}/2 pint/1^1/4 cups water
fresh coriander (cilantro) leaves, chopped
2 green chillies, finely chopped

1 Heat the oil in a large, heavy-based saucepan.

2 Add the white cumin seeds, mustard and onion seeds and dried red chillies to the saucepan, stirring well.

3 Add the tomatoes to the pan and stir-fry the mixture for 3-5 minutes.

4 Mix together the salt, ginger, garlic and chilli powder and spoon into the pan. Blend the whole mixture together.

5 Add the green beans and potatoes to the pan and stir-fry for about 5 minutes.

6 Add the water to the pan, reduce the heat and leave to simmer for 10-15 minutes, stirring occasionally.

7 Garnish the green bean and potato curry with chopped coriander (cilantro) leaves and green chillies and serve hot with cooked rice.

COOK'S TIP

Mustard seeds are often fried in oil or ghee to bring out their flavour before being combined with other ingredients.

Fried Cauliflower

A dry dish flavoured with a few herbs, this is a very versatile accompaniment.

Serves 4

INGREDIENTS

4 tbsp oil
1/2 tsp onion seeds
1/2 tsp mustard seeds
1/2 tsp fenugreek seeds

4 dried red chillies
1 small cauliflower, cut into small florets
1 tsp salt

1 green (bell) pepper, diced

1 Heat the oil in a large, heavy-based saucepan.

2 Add the onion seeds, mustard seeds, fenugreek seeds and the dried red chillies to the pan, stirring to mix.

3 Reduce the heat and gradually add all of the cauliflower and the salt to the pan. Stir-fry the mixture for 7-10 minutes, coating the cauliflower in the spice mixture.

4 Add the diced green (bell) pepper to the pan and stir-fry the mixture for 3-5 minutes.

5 Transfer the spicy fried cauliflower to a serving dish and serve hot.

VARIATION

For a weekend feast or a special occasion, this dish looks great made with baby cauliflowers instead of florets. Baby vegetables are more widely available nowadays, and the baby cauliflowers look very appealing on the plate. Peel off most of the outer leaves, leaving a few small leaves for decoration. Blanch the baby cauliflowers whole for 4 minutes and continue from step 3.

COOK'S TIP

Onion seeds are small and black. They may be labelled as kalonj in Asian food stores. Onion seeds can be used instead of pepper, but have a spicier and more bitter taste.

Aubergines (Eggplants) & Yogurt

This is an unusual dish, in that the aubergine (eggplant) is first baked in the oven, then cooked in a saucepan.

Serves 4

INGREDIENTS

2 medium aubergines (eggplants)	1 tsp white cumin seeds	3 tbsp natural yogurt
4 tbsp oil	1 tsp chilli powder	1/2 tsp mint sauce
1 medium onion, sliced	1 tsp salt	fresh mint leaves, to garnish

1 Rinse the aubergines (eggplants) and pat dry with paper towels.

2 Place the aubergines (eggplants) in an ovenproof dish. Bake in a pre-heated oven, 160°C/425°F/Gas Mark 3, for 45 minutes. Remove the baked aubergines (eggplants) from the oven and leave to cool.

3 Using a spoon, scoop out the aubergine (eggplant) flesh and reserve.

4 Heat the oil in a heavy-based saucepan. Add the onions and cumin seeds and fry, stirring for 1-2 minutes.

5 Add the chilli powder, salt, yogurt and the mint sauce to the pan and stir well to mix.

6 Add the aubergines (eggplants) to the onion and yogurt mixture and stir-fry for 5-7 minutes or until all of the liquid has been absorbed and the mixture is quite dry.

7 Transfer the aubergine (eggplant) and yogurt mixture to a serving dish and garnish with fresh mint leaves.

COOK'S TIP

Rich in protein and calcium, yogurt plays an important part in Indian cooking. Thick natural yogurt most closely resembles the yogurt made in many Indian homes.

Vegetable Kebabs (Kabobs)

If you invite several people to dinner or to a buffet meal nowadays there is a strong chance that one of them may be a vegetarian. These kebabs (kabobs) are easy to make and taste delicious.

Makes 10-12

INGREDIENTS

2 large potatoes, sliced
1 medium onion, sliced
1/2 medium cauliflower, cut into
   small florets
50 g/1³/4 oz peas
1 tbsp spinach purée (paste)

2-3 green chillies
fresh coriander (cilantro) leaves
1 tsp fresh ginger root, finely
   chopped
1 tsp fresh garlic, crushed
1 tsp ground coriander

1 pinch turmeric
1 tsp salt
50 g/1³/4 oz/1 cup breadcrumbs
300 ml/¹/2 pint/1¹/4 cups oil
fresh chilli strips, to garnish

1 Place the potatoes, onion and cauliflower florets in a pan of water and bring to the boil. Reduce the heat and leave to simmer until the potatoes are cooked through. Remove the vegetables from the pan with a perforated spoon and drain thoroughly.

2 Add the peas and spinach to the vegetables and mix, mashing down with a fork.

3 Using a sharp knife, finely chop the green chillies and fresh coriander (cilantro) leaves.

4 Mix the chillies and coriander (cilantro) with the ginger, garlic, ground coriander, turmeric and salt.

5 Blend the spice mixture into the vegetables, mixing with a fork to make a paste.

6 Scatter the breadcrumbs on to a large plate.

7 Break off 10-12 small balls from the spice paste. Flatten them with the palm of your hand to make flat, round shapes.

8 Dip each kebab (kabob) in the breadcrumbs, coating well.

9 Heat the oil in a heavy frying-pan (skillet) and shallow-fry the kabobs (kabobs), in batches, until golden brown, turning occasionally. Transfer to serving plates and garnish with fresh chilli strips. Serve hot.

Okra Curry

This is a delicious dry bhujia *(vegetarian curry) which should be served hot with Chapatis (see page 180). As okra is such a tasty vegetable it does not need many spices.*

Serves 4

INGREDIENTS

450 g/1 lb okra (lady's fingers)
150 ml/¹/₄ pint/²/₃ cup oil
2 medium onions, sliced

3 green chillies, finely chopped
2 curry leaves
1 tsp salt

1 tomato, sliced
2 tbsp lemon juice
fresh coriander (cilantro) leaves

1 Rinse the okra (lady's fingers) and drain thoroughly. Using a sharp knife, chop and discard the ends of the okra (lady's fingers). Cut the okra (lady's fingers) into 2.5 cm/1 inch long pieces.

2 Heat the oil in a large, heavy frying-pan (skillet). Add the onions, green chillies, curry leaves and salt and mix together. Stir-fry the vegetables for 5 minutes.

3 Gradually add the okra (lady's fingers), mixing in gently with a perforated spoon. Stir-fry the vegetable mixture over a medium heat for 12-15 minutes.

4 Add the sliced tomato to the pan and sprinkle over the lemon juice sparingly.

5 Garnish with coriander (cilantro) leaves, cover and leave to simmer for 3-5 minutes.

6 Transfer to serving plates and serve hot.

COOK'S TIP

Okra (lady's fingers) have a remarkable glutinous quality which naturally thickens curries and casseroles.

COOK'S TIP

When you buy fresh okra (lady's fingers), make sure they are not shriveled and that they do not have any brown spots. Fresh okra (lady's fingers) will keep, tightly wrapped, for up to 3 days in the refrigerator.

Spinach & Cheese Curry

This vegetarian curry is full of protein and iron. Serve as a side dish with meat curries or as part of a vegetarian menu. Panir is a type of cheese.

Serves 4

INGREDIENTS

300 ml/¹/₂ pint/1¹/₄ cups oil
200 g/7 oz panir, cubed (see Cook's Tip)

3 tomatoes, sliced
1 tsp ground cumin
1¹/₂ tsp ground chilli powder

1 tsp salt
400 g/14 oz spinach
3 green chillies

1 Heat the oil in a large frying pan (skillet). Add the cubed panir and fry, stirring occasionally, until golden brown.

2 Remove the panir from the frying pan (skillet) with a perforated spoon and leave to drain on kitchen paper.

3 Add the tomatoes to the remaining oil in the pan and stir-fry, breaking up the tomatoes, for 5 minutes.

4 Add the ground cumin, chilli powder and salt to the pan and mix together well.

5 Add the spinach to the pan and stir-fry over a low heat for 7-10 minutes.

6 Add the green chillies and the panir and cook, stirring, for a further 2 minutes.

7 Transfer to serving plates and serve hot with pooris or plain boiled rice.

VARIATION

You could used frozen spinach in this recipe. It should be thawed and squeezed dry before using.

COOK'S TIP

To make panir, boil 1 litre/ 1³/₄ pints/4¹/₂ cups milk slowly over a low heat, then add 2 tbsp lemon juice, stirring continuously and gently until the milk thickens and begins to curdle. Strain the curdled milk through a sieve. Set aside under a heavy weight for about 1¹/₂-2 hours to press to a flat shape about 1 cm/¹/₂ inch thick. Once set, the panir can be cut, like cheese, into whatever shape is required.

Stuffed Rice Pancakes

Dosas (pancakes) are widely eaten in southern India. They can be served either on their own with a chutney or as here with a vegetable filling, when they are known as masala dosa.

Makes 6–8

INGREDIENTS

200 g/7 oz rice and 50 g/1³/₄ oz *urid dhaal*, or 200 g/7 oz ground rice and 50 g/1³/₄ oz) *urid dhaal* flour (*ata*)
425–600 ml/³/₄–1 pint water
1 tsp salt
4 tbsp oil

FILLING:
4 medium potatoes, diced
3 green chillies, chopped
¹/₂ tsp turmeric
1 tsp salt
150 ml/¹/₄ pint/²/₃ cup oil
1 tsp mustard and onion seeds

3 dried chillies
4 curry leaves
2 tbsp lemon juice

1 To make the *dosas* (pancakes), soak the rice and *urid dhaal* for 3 hours. Grind the rice and *urid dhaal* to a smooth consistency, adding water if necessary. Set aside for a further 3 hours to ferment. Alternatively, if you are using ground rice and *urid dhaal* flour (*ata*), mix together in a bowl. Add the water and salt and stir until a batter is formed.

2 Heat about 1 tbsp of oil in a large, non-stick, frying-pan (skillet). Using a ladle, spoon the batter into the frying-pan (skillet). Tilt the frying-pan (skillet) to spread the mixture over the base. Cover and cook over a medium heat for about 2 minutes. Remove the lid and turn the *dosa* over very carefully. Pour a little oil around the edge, cover and cook for a further 2 minutes. Repeat with the remaining batter.

3 To make the filling, boil the potatoes in a pan of water. Add the chillies, turmeric and salt and cook until the potatoes are soft enough to be lightly mashed.

4 Heat the oil in a saucepan and fry the mustard and onion seeds, dried red chillies and curry leaves for about 1 minute. Pour the spice mixture over the mashed potatoes, then sprinkle over the lemon juice and mix well. Spoon the potato filling on one half of the *dosas* (pancakes) and fold the other half over the filling. Serve hot.

Potatoes with Spices & Onions

Masala aloo are potatoes cooked in spices and onions. Semi-dry when cooked, they make an excellent accompaniment to almost any meat or vegetable curry.

Serves 4

INGREDIENTS

6 tbsp oil
2 medium-sized onions, chopped finely
1 tsp fresh ginger root, finely chopped
1 tsp fresh garlic, crushed
1 tsp chilli powder
1¹/₂ tsp ground cumin

1¹/₂ tsp ground coriander
1 tsp salt
400 g/14 oz can new potatoes
1 tbsp lemon juice

BAGHAAR:
3 tbsp oil
3 dried red chillies

¹/₂ tsp onion seeds
¹/₂ tsp mustard seeds
¹/₂ tsp fenugreek seeds

TO GARNISH:
fresh coriander (cilantro) leaves
1 green chilli, finely chopped

1 Heat the oil in a large saucepan. Add the onions and fry, stirring, until golden brown. Reduce the heat, add the ginger, garlic, chilli powder, ground cumin, ground coriander and salt and stir-fry for about 1 minute. Remove the pan from the heat and set aside until required.

2 Drain the water from the potatoes. Add the potatoes to the onion mixture and spice mixture. Sprinkle over the lemon juice and mix well.

3 To make the *baghaar*, heat the oil in a separate pan. Add the red chillies, onion seeds, mustard seeds and fenugreek seeds and fry until the seeds turn a shade darker. Remove the pan from the heat and pour the *baghaar* over the potatoes.

4 Garnish with coriander (cilantro) leaves and chillies.

COOK'S TIP

You could also serve these spicy potatoes and onions, for a change, with roast lamb or lamb chops.

Mooli (White Radish) Curry

*This is rather an unusual recipe for a vegetarian curry. The
dish is good served hot with Chapatis (see page 180).*

Serves 4

INGREDIENTS

450 g/1 lb mooli (white radish),
  preferably with leaves
1 tbsp *moong dhaal*

600 ml/1 pint/2$^{1}/_{2}$ cups water
1 medium onion
150 ml/$^{1}/_{4}$ pint/$^{2}/_{3}$ cup oil

1 tsp fresh garlic, crushed
1 tsp red chillies, crushed
1 tsp salt

1 Rinse, peel and roughly slice
the mooli (white radish)
together with its leaves.

2 Place the mooli (white
radish), the leaves (if using)
and the *moong dhaal* in a pan and
pour over the water. Bring to the
boil until the mooli (white radish)
is soft enough to be handled.

3 Drain the mouli (white
radish) thoroughly and
squeeze out any excess water,
using your hands.

4 Using a sharp knife, slice the
onion thinly.

5 Heat the oil in a saucepan.
Add the onion, garlic, crushed
red chillies and salt and fry, stirring
occasionally, until the onions have
softened and turned a light golden
brown colour.

6 Stir the mooli (white radish)
mixture into the spiced onion
mixture and combine well. Reduce
the heat and continue cooking,
stirring frequently, for about
3-5 minutes.

7 Transfer the mooli (white
radish) curry to individual
serving plates and serve hot
with Chapatis (see page 180).

COOK'S TIP

*The vegetable used in this recipe,
mooli (white radish), looks a bit
like a parsnip without the tapering
end and is now sold in most
supermarkets as well as in Indian
and Pakistani grocers.*

Aubergines (Eggplants) in Pickling Spices

This is a very versatile dish that will go with almost anything and can be served warm or cold. Perfect as an 'extra' for a dinner party, this is another dish which originates from Hyderabad in southern India.

Serves 4

INGREDIENTS

2 tsp ground coriander
2 tsp ground cumin
2 tsp desiccated (shredded) coconut
2 tsp sesame seeds
1 tsp mixed mustard and onion seeds
300 ml/^{1}/$_2$ pint/1^1/$_4$ cups oil
3 medium onions, sliced
1 tsp fresh ginger root, finely chopped

1 tsp fresh garlic, crushed
^{1}/$_2$ tsp turmeric
1^1/$_2$ tsp chilli powder
1^1/$_2$ tsp salt
3 medium aubergines (eggplants), halved lengthwise
1 tbsp tamarind paste
300 ml/^{1}/$_2$ pint/1^1/$_4$ cups water

BAGHAAR:
1 tsp mixed onion and mustard seeds
1 tsp cumin seeds
4 dried red chillies
150 ml/^{1}/$_4$ pint/^{2}/$_3$ cup oil
coriander (cilantro) leaves
1 green chilli, finely chopped
3 hard-boiled (hard-cooked) eggs, halved, to garnish

1 Dry-roast the coriander, cumin, coconut, sesame seeds and mustard and onion seeds in a pan. Grind in a pestle and mortar or food processor and set aside.

2 Heat the oil in a frying pan (skillet) and fry the onions until golden. Reduce the heat and add the ginger, garlic, turmeric, chilli powder and salt, stirring. Leave to cool, then grind this mixture to form a paste.

3 Make 4 cuts across each aubergine (eggplant) half. Blend the spices with the onion paste. Spoon this mixture into the slits in the aubergines (eggplants).

4 In a bowl, mix the tamarind paste and 3 tbsp water to make a fine paste and set aside.

5 For the *baghaar*, fry the onion and mustard seeds, cumin seeds and chillies in the oil.

6 Reduce the heat and gently place the stuffed aubergines (eggplants) into the heated *baghaar* and stir gently. Stir in the tamarind paste and the rest of the water and cook over a medium heat for 15-20 minutes. Add the coriander (cilantro) and green chillies.

7 When cool, transfer to a serving dish and serve garnished with three halved hard-boiled eggs.

Dumplings in Yogurt Sauce

I use gram flour to flavour and thicken the sauce in this recipe, and add a baghaar *(seasoned oil dressing) just before serving. It makes a mouth-watering accompaniment to any meal.*

Serves 4

INGREDIENTS

DUMPLINGS:
100 g/3$^1/_2$ oz/$^3/_4$ cup gram flour
1 tsp chilli powder
$^1/_2$ tsp salt
$^1/_2$ tsp bicarbonate of soda (baking soda)
1 medium onion, finely chopped
2 green chillies
fresh coriander (cilantro) leaves
150 ml/$^1/_4$ pint/$^2/_3$ cup water
300 ml/$^1/_2$ pint/1$^1/_4$ cups oil

YOGURT SAUCE:
300 ml/$^1/_2$ pint/1$^1/_4$ cups yogurt
3 tbsp gram flour
150 ml/$^1/_4$ pint/$^2/_3$ cup water
1 tsp fresh ginger root, chopped
1 tsp fresh garlic, crushed
1$^1/_2$ tsp chilli powder
1$^1/_2$ tsp salt
$^1/_2$ tsp turmeric
1 tsp ground coriander
5 ml/1 tsp ground cumin

SEASONED DRESSING:
150 ml/$^1/_4$ pint/$^2/_3$ cup oil
1 tsp white cumin seeds
6 red dried chillies

1 To make the dumplings, sieve the gram flour into a large bowl. Add the chilli powder, salt, soda, onion, green chillies and coriander (cilantro) and mix. Add the water and mix to form a thick paste. Heat the oil in a frying-pan (skillet). Place teaspoonfuls of the paste in the oil and fry, turning once, over a medium heat until a crisp golden brown. Set aside.

2 To make the sauce, place the yogurt in a bowl and whisk with the gram flour and the water. Add all of the spices and mix well.

3 Push this mixture through a large sieve into a saucepan. Bring to a boil over a low heat, stirring continuously. If the yogurt sauce becomes too thick add a little extra water.

4 Pour the sauce into a deep serving dish and arrange all of the dumplings on top. Set aside and keep warm.

5 To make the dressing, heat the oil in a frying-pan (skillet). Add the white cumin seeds and the dried red chillies and fry until darker in colour. Pour the dressing over the dumplings and serve hot.

Potato Curry

Served hot with Pooris (see page 184), this curry makes an excellent brunch with Mango Chutney (see page 218) as an accompaniment.

Serves 4

INGREDIENTS

3 medium potatoes
150 ml/¹/₄ pint/²/₃ cup oil
1 tsp onion seeds
¹/₂ tsp fennel seeds

4 curry leaves
1 tsp ground cumin
1 tsp ground coriander
1 tsp chilli powder

1 pinch turmeric
1 tsp salt
1¹/₂ tsp *aamchoor* (dried mango powder)

1 Peel and rinse the potatoes. Using a sharp knife, cut each potato into six slices.

2 Boil the potato slices in a saucepan of water until just cooked, but not mushy (test by piercing with a sharp knife or a skewer). Set aside until required.

3 In a separate saucepan heat the oil. Reduce the heat and add the onion seeds, fennel seeds and curry leaves, stirring.

4 Remove the pan from the heat and add the ground cumin, coriander, chilli powder, turmeric, salt and aamchoor (dried mango powder), stirring well to combine.

5 Return the pan to the heat and stir-fry the mixture for about 1 minute.

6 Pour this mixture over the cooked potatoes, mix together and stir-fry over a low heat for about 5 minutes.

7 Transfer the potato curry to serving dishes and serve immediately.

COOK'S TIP

Traditionally, Semolina Dessert (see page 244) is served to follow Potato Curry.

Courgettes (Zucchini) & Fenugreek Seeds

This delicious curry contains fenugreek seeds which have a beautiful aroma and a distinctive taste.

Serves 4

INGREDIENTS

6 tbsp oil
1 medium onion, finely chopped
3 green chillies, finely chopped
1 tsp fresh ginger root, chopped finely

1 tsp fresh garlic, crushed
1 tsp chilli powder
450 g/1 lb courgettes (zucchini), sliced

2 tomatoes, sliced
fresh coriander (cilantro) leaves, plus extra to garnish
2 tsp fenugreek seeds

1 Heat the oil in a large frying pan (skillet).

2 Add the onion, green chillies, ginger, garlic and chilli powder to the pan, stirring well to combine.

3 Add the sliced courgettes (zucchini) and the sliced tomatoes to the pan and stir-fry for 5-7 minutes.

4 Add the cilantro (coriander) and fenugreek seeds to the courgette (zucchini) mixture in the pan and stir-fry for 5 minutes.

5 Remove the pan from the heat and transfer the courgette (zucchini) and fenugreek seed mixture to serving dishes. Garnish and serve hot with Chapatis (see page 180).

COOK'S TIP

Both the leaves and seeds of fenugreek are used, but the stalks and root should be discarded, as they have a bitter taste. Fresh fenugreek is sold in bunches. Fenugreek seeds are flat and yellowish brown in colour.

VARIATION

You could use coriander seeds instead of the fenugreek seeds, if you prefer.

Green Pumpkin Curry

The Indian pumpkin used in this curry is long and green and sold by weight.
It can easily be bought from any Indian or Pakistani grocers.

Serves 4

INGREDIENTS

150 ml/^{1}/$_4$ pint/^{2}/$_3$ cup oil
2 medium-sized onions, sliced
^{1}/$_2$ tsp white cumin seeds
450 g/1 lb green pumpkin, cubed

1 tsp *aamchoor* (dried mango powder)
1 tsp fresh ginger root, finely chopped

1 tsp fresh garlic, crushed
1 tsp crushed red chilli
^{1}/$_2$ tsp salt
300 ml/^{1}/$_2$ pint/1^1/$_4$ cups water

1 Heat the oil in a large frying pan (skillet). Add the onions and cumin seeds and fry, stirring occasionally, until a light golden brown colour.

2 Add the cubed pumpkin to the pan and stir-fry for 3-5 minutes over a low heat.

3 Mix the aamchoor (dried mango powder), ginger, garlic, chilli and salt together.

4 Add the spice mixture to the onion mixture, stirring well to combine.

5 Add the water, cover and cook over a low heat for 10-15 minutes, stirring occasionally.

6 Transfer to serving plates and serve with Gram Flour Bread (see page 176).

COOK'S TIP

Cumin seeds are popular with Indian cooks because of their warm, pungent flavour and aroma. The seeds are sold whole or ground, and are usually included as one of the flavourings in garam masala.

VARIATION

You can use ordinary pumpkin for this recipe, if you prefer.

Potatoes & Peas

This quick and easy-to-prepare vegetarian dish can be served either as an accompaniment or on its own with Chapatis (see page 180).

Serves 2-4

INGREDIENTS

150 ml/¹/₄ pint/²/₃ cup oil
3 medium onions, sliced
1 tsp fresh garlic, crushed
1 tsp fresh ginger root, finely
   chopped

1 tsp chilli powder
¹/₂ tsp turmeric
1 tsp salt
2 fresh green chillies, finely chopped
300 ml/¹/₂ pint/1¹/₄ cups water

3 medium potatoes
100 g/3¹/₂ oz peas
fresh coriander (cilantro) leaves,
   to garnish

1 Heat the oil in a large frying pan (skillet).

2 Add the onions to the frying pan (skillet) and fry, stirring occasionally, until the onions are golden brown.

3 Mix together the garlic, ginger, chilli powder, turmeric, salt and fresh green chillies. Add the spice mixture to the onions in the pan.

4 Stir in 150 ml/¹/₄ pint/²/₃ cup of the water, cover and cook until the onions are cooked through.

5 Meanwhile, cut the potatoes into six slices each, using a sharp knife.

6 Add the potato slices to the mixture in the pan and stir-fry for 5 minutes.

7 Add the peas and the remaining 150 ml/¹/₄ pint/ ²/₃ cup of the water to the pan, cover and cook for 7-10 minutes.

8 Transfer the potatoes and peas to serving plates and serve garnished with fresh coriander (cilantro) leaves.

COOK'S TIP

Turmeric is an aromatic root which is dried and ground to produce the distinctive bright yellow-orange powder used in many Indian dishes. It has a warm, aromatic smell and a full, somewhat musty taste.

Chick-pea (Garbanzo Bean) Curry

This curry is very popular amongst the many vegetarian people in India. There are many different ways of cooking chick-peas (garbanzo beans), but this version is probably one of the most delicious.

Serves 4

INGREDIENTS

6 tbsp oil
2 medium onions, sliced
1 tsp fresh ginger root, finely chopped
1 tsp ground cumin

1 tsp ground coriander
1 tsp fresh garlic, crushed
1 tsp chilli powder
2 fresh green chillies
fresh coriander (cilantro) leaves

150 ml/^{1}/$_4$ pint/^{2}/$_3$ cup water
1 large potato
400 g/14 oz can chick-peas (garbanzo beans), drained
1 tbsp lemon juice

1 Heat the oil in a large saucepan.

2 Add the onions to the pan and fry, stirring occasionally, until golden brown.

3 Reduce the heat, add the ginger, ground cumin, ground coriander, garlic, chilli powder, fresh green chillies and fresh coriander (cilantro) leaves to the pan and stir-fry for 2 minutes.

4 Add the water to the mixture in the pan and stir to mix.

5 Using a sharp knife, cut the potato into small dice.

6 Add the potatoes and the drained chick peas to the mixture in the pan, cover and leave to simmer, stirring occasionally, for 5-7 minutes.

7 Sprinkle the lemon juice over the curry.

8 Transfer the chick pea curry to serving dishes. Serve the curry hot with chapati, if you wish.

COOK'S TIP

Using canned chick-peas (garbanzo beans) saves time, but you can use dried chick-peas (garbanzo beans) if you prefer. Soak them overnight, then boil them for 15-20 minutes or until soft.

Mixed Vegetables

This is one of my favourite vegetarian recipes. You can make it with any vegetables you choose, but I think the combination below is ideal.

Serves 4

INGREDIENTS

300 ml/¹/₂ pint/1¹/₄ cups oil
1 tsp mustard seeds
1 tsp onion seeds
¹/₂ tsp white cumin seeds
3-4 curry leaves, chopped
450 g/1 lb onions, finely chopped
3 medium tomatoes, chopped

¹/₂ red, ¹/₂ green (bell) pepper, sliced
1 tsp fresh ginger root, finely chopped
1 tsp fresh garlic, crushed
1 tsp chilli powder
¹/₄ tsp turmeric
1 tsp salt
425 ml/³/₄ pint/2 cups water

2 medium potatoes, peeled and cut into pieces
¹/₂ cauliflower, cut into small florets
4 medium carrots, peeled and sliced
3 green chillies, finely chopped
fresh coriander (cilantro) leaves
1 tbsp lemon juice

1 Heat the oil in a large saucepan. Add the mustard, onion and white cumin seeds along with the curry leaves and fry until they turn a shade darker.

2 Add the onions to the pan and fry over a medium heat until golden brown.

3 Add the tomatoes and (bell) peppers and stir-fry for about 5 minutes.

4 Add the ginger, garlic, chilli powder, turmeric and salt and mix well.

5 Add 300 ml/¹/₂ pint/1¹/₄ cups of the water, cover and leave to simmer for 10-12 minutes, stirring occasionally.

6 Add the potatoes, cauliflower, carrots, green chillies and coriander (cilantro) leaves and stir-fry for about 5 minutes.

7 Add the remaining 150 ml/ ¹/₄ pint/²/₃ cup of water and the lemon juice, stirring to combine. Cover and leave to simmer for about 15 minutes, stirring occasionally.

8 Transfer the mixed vegetables to serving plates and serve immediately.

Potato & Cauliflower Curry

Potatoes and cauliflower go very well together. Served with a dhaal *and Pooris (see page 184), this dish makes a perfect vegetarian meal.*

Serves 4

INGREDIENTS

150 ml/^{1}/$_4$ pint/^{2}/$_3$ cup oil
^{1}/$_2$ tsp white cumin seeds
4 dried red chillies
2 medium onions, sliced
1 tsp fresh ginger root, finely chopped

1 tsp fresh garlic, crushed
1 tsp chilli powder
1 tsp salt
1 pinch of turmeric
3 medium potatoes

^{1}/$_2$ cauliflower, cut into small florets
2 green chillies (optional)
fresh coriander (cilantro) leaves
150 ml/^{1}/$_4$ pint/^{2}/$_3$ cup water

1 Heat the oil in a large saucepan.

2 Add the white cumin seeds and dried red chillies to the pan, stirring to mix.

3 Add the onions to the pan and fry, stirring occasionally, until golden brown.

4 Mix the ginger, garlic, chilli powder, salt and turmeric together. Add the spice mixture to the onions and stir-fry for about 2 minutes.

5 Add the potatoes and cauliflower to the onion and spice mixture, stirring to coat the vegetables in the spice mixture.

6 Reduce the heat and add the green chillies (if using), fresh coriander (cilantro) leaves and water to the pan. Cover and leave the mixture to simmer for about 10-15 minutes.

7 Transfer the potato and cauliflower curry to warm serving plates and serve immediately.

COOK'S TIP

Always handle chillies with caution, preferably wearing rubber gloves because the juices are extremely pungent. Wash your hands thoroughly after preparing and handling chillies and do not allow your fingers near your eyes as this can be very painful.

Dry Split Okra

This is an unusual way of cooking this delicious vegetable. The dish is dry when cooked, and should be served hot with Chapatis (see page 180) and a dhaal.

Serves 4

INGREDIENTS

450 g/1 lb okra
150 ml/¹/₄ pint/²/₃ cup oil
100 g/3¹/₂ oz/¹/₂ cup dried onions

2 tsp *aamchoor* (dried mango powder)
1 tsp ground cumin

1 tsp chilli powder
1 tsp salt

1 Prepare the okra by cutting the ends off and discarding them. Carefully split the okra down the middle without cutting through completely.

2 Heat the oil in a large saucepan. Add the dried onions and fry until crisp.

3 Remove the onions from the pan with a perforated spoon and leave to drain thoroughly on paper towels.

4 When cool enough to handle, roughly tear the dried onions and place in a large bowl.

5 Add the *aamchoor* (dried mango), ground cumin, chilli powder and salt to the dried onions and blend well together.

6 Spoon the onion and spice mixture into the split okra.

7 Re-heat the oil in the saucepan.

8 Gently add the okra to the hot oil and cook over a low heat for about 10-12 minutes.

9 Transfer the cooked okra to a serving dish and serve immediately.

COOK'S TIP

Ground cumin has a warm, pungent aromatic flavour and is used extensively in Indian cooking. It is a good storecupboard standby.

Tomato Curry

This vegetarian tomato curry is served topped with a few hard-boiled eggs. It makes a lovely accompaniment to almost any meal, and goes well with Spiced Rice & Lentils (see page 154).

Serves 4

INGREDIENTS

400 g/14 oz can tomatoes
1 tsp fresh ginger root, chopped finely
1 tsp fresh garlic, crushed
1 tsp chilli powder
1 tsp salt
$^1/_2$ tsp ground coriander

$^1/_2$ tsp ground cumin
4 tbsp oil
$^1/_2$ tsp onion seeds
$^1/_2$ tsp mustard seeds
$^1/_2$ tsp fenugreek seeds
1 pinch white cumin seeds
3 dried red chillies

2 tbsp lemon juice
3 eggs, hard-boiled (hard-cooked)
fresh coriander (cilantro) leaves

1 Place the tomatoes in a large mixing bowl.

2 Add the ginger, garlic, chilli powder, salt, ground coriander and ground cumin to the tomatoes and blend well.

3 Heat the oil in a saucepan. Add the onion, mustard, fenugreek and white cumin seeds, and the dried red chillies, and stir-fry for about 1 minute. Remove the pan from the heat.

4 Add the tomato mixture to the spicy oil mixture and return to the heat. Stir-fry the mixture for about 3 minutes, then reduce the heat and cook with the lid ajar for 7-10 minutes, stirring occasionally.

5 Sprinkle over the lemon juice sparingly.

6 Transfer the tomato curry to a serving dish, set aside and keep warm until required.

7 Shell and halve the hard-boiled (hard-cooked) eggs, then gently add them, yolk end down, to the tomato curry.

8 Garnish with fresh coriander (cilantro) leaves and serve hot.

COOK'S TIP

This tomato curry can be made in advance and frozen, as it freezes particularly well.

Breads & Grains

The most common Indian breads are chapati, paratas and poori, all of which can be made with wholemeal flour – so they are very healthy foods. These three breads are cooked almost every day in most Indian households. Indian breads are made as individual portions, and I suggest you allow 2 per person.

Rice is served with almost every meal in India, so the Indians have created a variety of ways of cooking it. Whatever the dish, the aim is to produce dry, separate grained rice that is cooked yet still has some 'bite' to it. Basmati rice is the type I recommend, because it cooks very well and gives an excellent result. It is best to soak it for about 20-30 minutes before cooking, to prevent the grains from sticking to each other. As a rough guide, allow about 75 g/2³/4 oz rice per person.

There are at least 30 different types of lentil to be found in India, but the 4 most commonly used are moong, masoor, chana and urid. Rich in protein, lentils make ideal accompaniments to vegetable curries, which otherwise lack protein. Lentils are also delicious cooked with a variety of meats. Before cooking, wash the lentils at least twice and if you have time, soak them for 3 hours – this will also cut down on the cooking time.

Lemon Dhaal

This dhaal is eaten almost every day in most households in Hyderabad in India. Traditionally, it is cooked with tamarind but I like to use lemon juice instead, which is easier and more colourful.

Serves 4

INGREDIENTS

100 g/3¹/₂ oz/¹/₂ cup *masoor dhaal*
1 tsp fresh ginger root, finely chopped
1 tsp fresh garlic, crushed
1 tsp chilli powder
¹/₂ tsp turmeric

425 ml/³/₄ pint/2 cups water
1 tsp salt
3 tbsp lemon juice
2 green chillies
fresh coriander (cilantro) leaves

BAGHAAR:
150 ml/¹/₄ pint/²/₃ cup oil
4 whole garlic cloves
6 dried red chillies
1 tsp white cumin seeds

1 Rinse the *masoor dhaal* and place in a large saucepan.

2 Add the ginger, garlic, chilli powder and turmeric to the dhaal. Stir in 300 ml/¹/₂ pint/ 1¹/₄ cups of the water and bring to a boil over a medium heat with the lid left slightly ajar until the *dhaal* is soft enough to be mashed.

3 Mash the *dhaal*. Add the salt, lemon juice and 150 ml/ ¹/₄ pint/²/₃ cup of the water, stir and mix well. It should be of a fairly smooth consistency.

4 Add the green chillies and fresh coriander (cilantro) leaves to the *dhaal* and set aside.

5 To make the *baghaar*, heat the oil in a pan. Add the garlic, red chillies and white cumin seeds and fry for about 1 minute. Turn off the heat, then when the heat has been reduced pour the *baghaar* over the *dhaal*. If the *dhaal* is too runny cook over a medium heat with the lid off for 3-5 minutes.

6 Transfer to a serving dish and serve hot.

COOK'S TIP

This dish is a good accompaniment to Beef Khorma with Almonds (see page 50).

White Lentils

This dhaal *is dry when cooked, so I always give it a* baghaar *(seasoned oil dressing).*
It makes an excellent accompaniment to any meal of khorma *and Chapatis (see page 180).*

Serves 2–4

INGREDIENTS

100 g/3¹/₂ oz/¹/₂ cup *urid dhaal*
1 tsp fresh ginger root, finely
   chopped
600 ml/1 pint/2¹/₂ cups water

1 tsp salt
1 tsp pepper
2 tbsp pure or vegetable ghee
2 cloves garlic, peeled

2 red chillies, finely chopped
fresh mint leaves, to garnish

1 Rinse the lentils twice, removing any stones.

2 Place the lentils and ginger in a large saucepan.

3 Add the water and bring to a boil, covered, over a medium heat for about 30 minutes. Check to see whether the lentils are cooked by rubbing them between your finger and thumb. If they are still a little hard in the middle, cook for a further 5-7 minutes. If necessary, remove the lid and cook until any remaining water has evaporated.

4 Add the salt and coarsely ground black pepper to the lentils, mix well and set aside.

5 Heat the ghee in a separate saucepan. Add the cloves of garlic and chopped red chillies, and stir well to mix.

6 Pour the garlic and chilli mixture over the lentils and then garnish with the fresh mint leaves.

7 Transfer the white lentils to serving dishes and serve hot with Chapatis (see page 180).

COOK'S TIP

Urid dhaal *are small, round white split lentils, which are popular with northern Indians.* Dhaals *are usually labelled simply 'lentils' in most supermarkets.*

Onion Dhaal

This dhaal *is semi-dry when cooked so it is best to serve it with a curry which has a sauce.
Ordinary onions can be used as a substitute if spring onions (scallions) are not available.*

Serves 4

INGREDIENTS

100 g/3^1/$_2$ oz/^{1}/$_2$ cup *masoor dhaal*
6 tbsp oil
1 small bunch spring onions
  (scallions), trimmed and chopped,
  including the green part

1 tsp fresh ginger root, finely
  chopped
1 tsp fresh garlic, crushed
^{1}/$_2$ tsp chilli powder
^{1}/$_2$ tsp turmeric

300 ml/^{1}/$_2$ pint/1^1/$_4$ cups water
1 tsp salt
1 fresh green chilli, finely chopped
fresh coriander (cilantro) leaves

1 Rinse the lentils and set aside until required.

2 Heat the oil in a saucepan. Add the spring onions (scallions) to the pan and fry until lightly browned.

3 Reduce the heat and add the ginger, garlic, chilli powder and turmeric to the pan. Stir-fry the spring onions (scallions) with the spices.

4 Add the lentils and mix to blend together.

5 Add the water to the lentil mixture in the pan, reduce the heat further and cook for 20-25 minutes.

6 When the lentils are cooked thoroughly, add the salt and stir with a wooden spoon to gently combine.

7 Garnish the onion lentils with the chopped green chillies and fresh coriander (cilantro) leaves. Transfer the onion lentils to a serving dish and serve immediately.

COOK'S TIP

Masoor dhaal *are small, round, pale orange split lentils. They turn a pale yellow colour when cooked.*

Oil-Dressed Dhaal

This dhaal *is given a* tarka, *or* baghaar *(seasoned oil dressing), just before serving, of ghee, onion and a combination of seeds. It has a thick sauce when cooked.*

Serves 4

INGREDIENTS

75 g/2³/4 oz/5 tbsp *masoor dhaal*
50 g/1³/4 oz/4 tbsp *moong dhaal*
450 ml/³/4 pint/2 cups water
1 tsp fresh ginger root, finely
   chopped
1 tsp fresh garlic, crushed

2 red chillies, chopped
1 tsp salt

TARKA (BAGHAAR):
2 tbsp ghee
1 medium onion, sliced

mixed mustard and onion seeds

1 Rinse the lentils, removing any stones.

2 Place the lentils in a large saucepan and pour over the water, stirring. Add the ginger, garlic and red chillies and bring to a boil over a medium heat, half covered with a lid, until they are soft enough to be mashed (about 15-20 minutes).

3 Mash the lentils and add more water if necessary to form a thick sauce.

4 Add the salt to the lentil mixture and stir to combine. Transfer the lentils to a heatproof serving dish.

5 Just before serving, melt the ghee in a small saucepan. Add the onion and fry until golden brown. Add the mustard and onion seeds and stir to mix.

6 Pour the onion mixture over the lentils while still hot. Transfer to a serving dish and serve immediately.

COOK'S TIP

This dish makes a a very good accompaniment, especially for a dry vegetarian or meat curry. It also freezes well – simply re-heat it in a saucepan or covered in the oven.

Black-Eye Beans (Peas)

This is semi-dry when cooked, and is very good served with a few drops of lemon juice or with Chapatis (see page 180) and a wet curry.

Serves 4

INGREDIENTS

150 g/5¹/2 oz/1 cup black-eye beans (peas)
300 ml/¹/2 pint/1¹/4 cups oil
2 medium onions, sliced
1 tsp fresh ginger root, finely chopped

1 tsp fresh garlic, crushed
1 tsp chilli powder
1¹/2 tsp salt
1¹/2 tsp ground coriander
1¹/2 tsp ground cumin
150 ml/¹/4 pint/²/3 cup water

2 green chillies
fresh coriander (cilantro) leaves
1 tbsp lemon juice

1 Rinse and soak the black-eye beans (peas) in a bowl of water overnight.

2 Place the black-eye beans (peas) in a pan of water and bring to a boil over a low heat for about 30 minutes. Drain the beans (peas) thoroughly and set aside.

3 Heat the oil in a pan. Add the onions and fry until golden brown. Add the ginger, garlic, chilli powder, salt, ground coriander and ground cumin and stir-fry the mixture for 3-5 minutes.

4 Add the water to the pan, cover and cook the mixture until all of the water has completely evaporated.

5 Add the boiled black-eye beans (peas), green chillies and coriander (cilantro) leaves to the onions and stir to blend together. Stir-fry the bean (pea) mixture for 3-5 minutes.

6 Transfer the black-eye beans (peas) to a serving dish and sprinkle over the lemon juice. Serve hot or cold.

COOK'S TIP

Black-eye beans (peas) are oval-shaped, grey or beige beans (peas) with a dark dot in the centre. They have a slightly smoky flavour. They are sold canned as well as dried.

Dry Moong Dhaal

I like to give this dhaal *a* baghaar *(seasoned oil dressing) of butter, dried red chillies and white cumin seeds. It is simple to cook and tastes very good.*

Serves 4

INGREDIENTS

150 g/5¹/₂ oz/1 cup *moong dhaal*
1 tsp fresh ginger root, finely
   chopped
¹/₂ tsp ground cumin
¹/₂ tsp ground coriander

1 tsp fresh garlic, crushed
¹/₂ tsp chilli powder
600 ml/1 pint/2¹/₂ cups water
1 tsp salt

BAGHAAR:
100 g/3¹/₂ oz/8 tbsp unsalted butter
5 dried red chillies
1 tsp white cumin seeds

1 Rinse the lentils, removing any stones.

2 Place the lentils in a pan. Add the ginger, ground cumin, ground coriander, garlic and chilli powder, and stir to mix.

3 Pour in the water to cover the lentil mixture. Cook over a medium heat, stirring, until the lentils are soft but not mushy.

4 Add the salt to the lentils and stir to mix. Transfer to a serving dish and keep warm.

5 Meanwhile, make the *baghaar*. Melt the butter in a saucepan. Add the dried red chillies and white cumin seeds and fry until they begin to pop.

6 Pour the *baghaar* over the lentils and serve hot with chapati and a vegetable or meat curry.

COOK'S TIP

Dried red chillies are the quickest way to add heat to a dish.

COOK'S TIP

Moong dhaal *are tear-drop-shaped yellow split lentils, more popular in northern India than in the south.*

Spinach & Chana Dhaal

An attractive-looking dish, this makes a good vegetarian accompaniment to almost any meal.
For a good contrast in colour and taste, I usually cook a Tomato Curry (see page 134) with this.

Serves 4–6

INGREDIENTS

4 tbsp *chana dhaal*
6 tbsp oil
1 tsp mixed onion and mustard seeds
4 dried red chillies

400-450 g/14-16 oz can spinach, drained
1 tsp fresh ginger root, chopped finely
1 tsp ground coriander

1 tsp ground cumin
1 tsp salt
1 tsp chilli powder
2 tbsp lemon juice
1 green chilli, to garnish

1 Soak the *chana dhaal* in a bowl of warm water for at least 3 hours, preferably overnight.

2 Place the lentils in a saucepan, cover with water and boil for 30 minutes.

3 Heat the oil in a saucepan. Add the mixed onion and mustard seeds and dried red chillies and fry, stirring constantly, until they turn a shade darker.

4 Add the drained spinach to the pan, mixing gently.

5 Add the ginger, ground coriander, ground cumin, salt and chilli powder to the mixture in the pan. Reduce the heat and gently stir-fry the mixture for 7-10 minutes.

6 Add the lentils to the pan and blend into the spinach mixture well, stirring gently so that it does not break up.

7 Transfer the mixture to a serving dish. Sprinkle over the lemon juice and garnish with the green chilli. Serve immediately.

COOK'S TIP

Very similar in appearance to moong dhaal – the yellow split peas – chana dhaal has slightly less shiny grains. It is used as a binding agent and may be bought from Indian and Pakistani grocers.

Strained Dhaal with Meatballs

This is a dhaal with a difference. After cooking it I put meatballs (koftas) in it and a few fried potato wafers. Serve it with Fried Spicy Rice (see page 160) or plain boiled rice and poppadoms.

Serves 6-8

INGREDIENTS

200 g/7 oz/1¹/₂ cups *masoor dhaal*
1 tsp fresh ginger root, crushed
1 tsp fresh garlic, crushed
¹/₂ tsp turmeric
1¹/₂ tsp chilli powder
1¹/₂ tsp salt
3 tbsp lemon juice
850 ml/1¹/₂ pints/3³/₄ cups water

TO GARNISH:
3 green chillies, finely chopped
fresh coriander (cilantro) leaves,
    chopped

BAGHAAR:
150 ml/¹/₄ pint/²/₃ cup oil
3 garlic cloves

4 dried red chillies
1 tsp white cumin seeds

POTATO FRIES:
pinch of salt
2 medium potatoes, sliced thinly
300 ml/¹/₂ pint/1¹/₄ cups oil

1 Rinse the lentils, removing any stones.

2 Place the lentils in a saucepan and cover with 600 ml/1 pint/ 2½ cups water. Add the ginger, garlic, turmeric and chilli powder and boil until the lentils are soft and mushy. Add the salt, stirring.

3 Mash the lentils, then push them through a sieve, reserving the liquid. Add the lemon juice to the strained liquid.

4 Stir 300 ml/½ pint/1¼ cups of the water into the strained liquid and bring to the boil over a low heat. Set aside.

5 To make the meatballs, follow the recipe for Beef Kebabs (Kabobs) on page 46, but use the reserved strained liquid instead of water and in addition, shape the mixture into small balls rather than flat rounds. Drop the meatballs gently into the lentil mixture.

6 Prepare the *baghaar*. Heat the oil in a pan. Add the garlic, dried red chillies and white cumin seeds and fry for 2 minutes. Pour the *baghaar* over the lentil mixture, stirring to mix.

7 For the potato fries, rub the salt over the potato slices. Heat the oil in a frying pan (skillet) and fry the potatoes, turning, until crisp. Garnish the meatballs with the fried potatoes, chillies and coriander (cilantro).

Spiced Rice & Lentils

This is a lovely combination of rice and masoor dhaal, *simple to cook and delicious served with minced lamb and chutney. When I serve this, I like to add a knob of unsalted butter.*

Serves 4

INGREDIENTS

200 g/7 oz/1 cup basmati rice
175 g/6 oz/³⁄₄ cup *masoor dhaal*
2 tbsp pure or vegetable ghee

1 small onion, sliced
1 tsp fresh ginger root, finely chopped

1 tsp fresh garlic, crushed
¹⁄₂ tsp turmeric
600 ml/1 pint/2¹⁄₂ cups water
1 tsp salt

1 Combine the rice and *dhaal* and rinse twice, rubbing with your fingers, and removing any stones. Set aside until required.

2 Heat the ghee in a large saucepan. Add the onion and fry, stirring occasionally, for about 2 minutes.

3 Reduce the heat, add the ginger, garlic, and turmeric and stir-fry for 1 minute.

4 Add the rice and *dhaal* to the mixture in the pan and blend together, mixing gently.

5 Add the water to the mixture in the pan and bring to the boil. Reduce the heat and cook, covered, for 20-25 minutes.

6 Just before serving, add the salt and mix to combine.

7 Transfer the spiced rice and lentils to a serving dish and serve immediately.

VARIATION

Moong dhaal *may be substituted for* masoor dhaal *in this recipe.*

COOK'S TIP

Many Indian recipes specify using ghee as the cooking fat. This is because it is similar to clarified butter in that it can be heated to a very high temperature without burning. Ghee adds a nutty flavour to dishes and a glossy shine to sauces. You can buy ghee in cans, and a vegetarian version is also available. Store at room temperature or keep in the refrigerator.

Chana Dhaal Cooked with Rice

*I use saffron for this dish, which makes it rather special. It is delicious served
with any Raita (see page 216) and a meat curry such as Spicy Lamb Curry (see page 40).*

Serves 6

INGREDIENTS

100 g/3½ oz/¾ cup *chana dhaal*
60 ml/4 tbsp ghee
2 medium onions, sliced
1 tsp fresh ginger root, finely
    chopped
1 tsp fresh garlic, crushed
½ tsp turmeric

2 tsp salt
½ tsp chilli powder
1 tsp garam masala
5 tbsp yogurt
1.35 litres/2¼ pints/5⅔ cups water
150 ml/¼ pint/⅔ cup milk
1 tsp saffron

3 tbsp lemon juice
2 green chillies
fresh coriander (cilantro) leaves
3 black cardamoms
3 black cumin seeds
450 g/1 lb/2¼ cups basmati rice

1 Rinse and soak the *chana dhaal* for 3 hours. Rinse the rice, removing any stones and set aside.

2 Heat the ghee in a frying pan (skillet). Add the onion and fry until golden brown. Using a perforated spoon, remove half of the onion with a little of the ghee and set aside in a bowl.

3 Add the ginger, garlic, turmeric, 1 tsp of the salt, the chilli powder and garam masala to the mixture remaining in the pan and stir-fry for 5 minutes. Stir in the yogurt and add the *chana dhaal* and 150 ml/¼ pint/⅔ cup water. Cook, covered, for 15 minutes. Set aside.

4 Meanwhile, boil the milk with the saffron and set aside with the reserved fried onion, lemon juice, green chillies and coriander (cilantro) leaves.

5 Boil the rest of the water and add the salt, black cardamoms, black cumin seeds and the rice, and cook, stirring, until the rice is half-cooked. Drain, and place half of the fried onion, saffron, lemon juice, green chillies and coriander (cilantro) on top of the *chana dhaal* mixture. Place the remaining rice on top of this and the rest of the fried onion, saffron, lemon juice, chillies and coriander (cilantro) on top of the rice. Cover tightly with a lid and cook for 20 minutes over a very low heat. Mix with a slotted spoon before serving.

Pulao Rice

Plain boiled rice is eaten by most people in India every day, but for entertaining we tend to choose a more interesting rice dish, such as this one which has different-coloured grains and spices in it.

Serves 2-4

INGREDIENTS

200 g/7 oz/1 cup basmati rice
2 tbsp ghee
3 green cardamoms
2 cloves

3 peppercorns
1/2 tsp salt
1/2 tsp saffron

400 ml/3/4 pint/2 cups water

1 Rinse the rice twice and set aside until required.

2 Heat the ghee in a saucepan. Add the cardamoms, cloves and peppercorns to the pan and fry, stirring, for about 1 minute.

3 Add the rice and stir-fry for a further 2 minutes.

4 Add the salt, saffron and water to the rice mixture and reduce the heat. Cover the pan and leave to simmer over a low heat until the water has evaporated.

5 Transfer to a serving dish and serve hot.

COOK'S TIP

The most expensive of all spices, saffron strands are the stamens of a type of crocus. They give dishes a rich, golden colour, as well as adding a distinctive, slightly bitter taste. Saffron is sold as a powder or in strands. Saffron strands are more expensive, but do have a superior flavour. Some books recommend substituting turmeric – although the colours are similar, the tastes are not.

COOK'S TIP

Cloves should be used with caution because the flavour can be overwhelming if too many are used.

Fried Spicy Rice

I use ginger and garlic for this beautifully aromatic rice dish, which gives it a lovely flavour. If desired, you can add a few peas to it for extra colour and variety.

Serves 4–6

INGREDIENTS

450 g/1 lb/2¼ cups rice
1 medium onion
2 tbsp ghee
1 tsp fresh ginger root, finely chopped

1 tsp fresh garlic, crushed
1 tsp salt
1 tsp black cumin seeds
3 whole cloves

3 whole green cardamoms
2 cinnamon sticks
4 peppercorns
750 ml/1¼ pints/3¼ cups water

1 Rinse the rice, removing any stones.

2 Using a sharp knife, cut the onion into slices.

3 Melt the ghee in a large saucepan and fry the onion until a crisp golden brown colour.

4 Add the ginger, garlic and salt to the onions in the pan, stirring to combine.

5 Remove half of the spicy onions from the saucepan and set aside.

6 Add the rice, black cumin seeds, cloves, cardamoms, cinnamon sticks and peppercorns to the mixture in the pan and stir-fry for 3-5 minutes.

7 Add the water to the mixture in the pan and bring to the boil. Reduce the heat, cover and cook until steam comes out through the lid. Check to see whether the rice is cooked.

8 Transfer the fried spicy rice to a serving dish and serve garnished with the reserved fried onions.

COOK'S TIP

Cardamom pods contain numerous tiny black seeds which have a warm flavour and are highly aromatic – green cardamoms are considered the best because of their fine delicate flavour. Green cardamoms are also prized for their digestive properties, and some Indians chew them raw after they have eaten extra-spicy curries, to aid digestion and sweeten the breath.

Vegetable Pulao

*This is a lovely way of cooking rice and vegetables together, and the saffron
gives it a beautiful aroma. Serve this with a Raita (see page 216) and any kebab (kabob) dish.*

Serves 4–6

INGREDIENTS

2 medium potatoes, each peeled and
  cut into 6

1 medium aubergine (eggplant), cut
  into 6

200 g/7 oz carrots, peeled and sliced

50 g/1¾ oz green beans, cut into
  pieces

4 tbsp ghee

2 medium onions, sliced

175 ml/6 fl oz/¾ cup yogurt

2 tsp fresh ginger root, finely
  chopped

2 tsp fresh garlic, crushed

2 tsp garam masala

2 tsp black cumin seeds

½ tsp turmeric

3 black cardamoms

3 cinnamon sticks

2 tsp salt

1 tsp chilli powder

600 g/1½ lb/3 cups basmati rice

5 tbsp lemon juice

½ tsp saffron strands, boiled in
  300 ml/½ pint/1¼ cups milk

TO GARNISH:

4 green chillies, chopped

fresh coriander (cilantro) leaves,
  chopped

1 Prepare the vegetables. Heat
the ghee in a pan (skillet) and
fry the potatoes, aubergine
(eggplant), carrots and beans,
turning. Remove from the pan
and set aside. Fry the onions until
soft and add the yogurt, ginger,
garlic, garam masala, 1 tsp
black cumin seeds, turmeric,
1 cardamom, 1 cinnamon stick,
1 tsp salt and the chilli powder
and stir-fry for 3-5 minutes.
Return the vegetables to the pan
and fry for 4-5 minutes.

2 Prepare the saffron mixture. In
a pan of boiling water, half-
cook the rice with 1 tsp salt, 2
cinnamon sticks, 2 black cardamoms
and 1 tsp black cumin seeds. Drain
the rice, leaving half in the pan while
transferring the other half to a bowl.

Pour the vegetable mixture on top of
the rice in the pan. Pour half of the
lemon juice and half of the saffron
in milk over the vegetables and rice,
cover with the remaining rice and
pour the remaining lemon juice and
saffron in milk over the top. Garnish
with chillies and coriander
(cilantro), return to the heat and
cover. Cook over a low heat for
about 20 minutes. Serve hot.

Brown Rice with Fruit & Nuts

Here is a tasty and filling rice dish that is nice and spicy and includes fruits for a refreshing flavour and toasted nuts for an interesting crunchy texture.

Serves 4-6

INGREDIENTS

4 tbsp vegetable ghee or oil
1 large onion, chopped
2 garlic cloves, crushed
2.5 cm/1 inch ginger root, chopped finely
1 tsp chilli powder
1 tsp cumin seeds

1 tbsp mild or medium curry powder or paste
300 g/10 oz/1^1/$_2$ cups brown rice
850 ml/1^1/$_2$ pints/3^1/$_2$ cups boiling vegetable stock
400 g/14 oz can chopped tomatoes
175 g/6 oz ready-soaked dried apricots or peaches, cut into slivers

1 red (bell) pepper, cored, seeded and diced
90 g/3 oz frozen peas
1-2 small, slightly green bananas
60-90 g/2-3oz/^{1}/$_3$-^{1}/$_2$ cup toasted mixed nuts
salt and pepper

1 Heat the ghee or oil in a large saucepan, add the onion and fry gently for 3 minutes.

2 Stir in the garlic, ginger, chilli powder, cumin seeds, curry powder or paste and rice. Cook gently for 2 minutes, stirring all the time, until the rice is coated in the spiced oil.

3 Pour in the boiling stock, stirring to mix. Add the tomatoes and season with salt and pepper to taste. Bring the mixture to the boil, then reduce the heat, cover the pan and leave to simmer gently for 40 minutes or until the rice is almost cooked and most of the liquid is absorbed.

4 Add the apricots or peaches, red (bell) pepper and peas to the rice mixture in the pan. Cover and continue cooking for 10 minutes.

5 Remove the pan from the heat and leave to stand for 5 minutes without uncovering.

6 Peel and slice the bananas. Uncover the rice mixture and toss with a fork to mix. Add the toasted nuts and sliced banana and toss lightly.

7 Transfer the brown rice and fruit and nuts to a serving platter and serve hot.

Prawn (Shrimp) Pulao

This recipe features caraway seeds, which give a distinctive taste and aroma to this unusual prawn (shrimp) pulao. Serve with a Raita (see page 216) and Beef Kebabs (kabobs) (see page 46).

Serves 4

INGREDIENTS

450 g/1 lb frozen prawns (shrimp)
1/2 tsp saffron
150 ml/1/2 pint/1 1/4 cups milk
1 tsp chilli powder
1 1/2 tsp caraway seeds

2 cinnamon sticks
2 green cardamoms
2 medium onions, sliced
2 bay leaves
1 tsp fresh ginger root, finely chopped

5 ml/1 tsp salt
450 g/1 lb/2 1/4 cups basmati rice
5 tbsp ghee
4 tbsp lemon juice
fresh mint leaves, plus extra to garnish

1 Defrost the prawns by placing them in a bowl of cold water.

2 Prepare the saffron by boiling 150 ml/1/4 pint/2/3 cup of the milk in a pan and adding the saffron. Set aside until required.

3 Place the chilli powder, 1 tsp caraway seeds, cinnamon sticks, green cardamoms, 1 sliced onion, the bay leaves, ginger and salt in a pestle and mortar and grind to a fine paste. Set aside.

4 Place the rice in a saucepan of boiling water and when the rice is half-cooked, remove from the heat and set aside.

5 Heat the ghee in a pan and fry the remaining onion until golden brown. Transfer the onions to a bowl and mix with the lemon juice and a few mint leaves.

6 Add the spice paste and prawns (shrimps) to the pan and stir-fry for about 5 minutes. Remove the prawns (shrimps) and spices and place in a bowl.

7 Place the half-cooked rice in a saucepan and pour the prawn (shrimp) mixture over the top. Pour half of the onion and lemon mixture and half of the saffron mixture over the prawns (shrimp). Arrange the other half of the rice on top and pour over the remaining ingredients.

8 Add the extra mint leaves, cover and cook over a low heat for 15-20 minutes.

9 Mix well before transferring to a serving dish.

Chicken Biryani

This biryani recipe may look rather complicated, but is not difficult to follow. You can substitute lamb for chicken, if you prefer, but you would have to marinate it overnight.

Serves 6

INGREDIENTS

1¹/₂ tsp fresh ginger root, finely chopped
1¹/₂ tsp fresh garlic, crushed
1 tbsp garam masala
1 tsp chilli powder
¹/₂ tsp turmeric
2 tsp salt
20 crushed green/white cardamom seeds, crushed

300 ml/10 fl oz/1¹/₄ cups natural yogurt
1.5 kg/3 lb 5 oz chicken, skinned and cut into 8
150 ml/¹/₄ pint/²/₃ cup milk
¹/₂ tsp saffron strands
6 tbsp ghee
2 medium onions, sliced
450 g/1 lb/2¹/₄ cups basmati rice

2 cinnamon sticks
4 black peppercorns
1 tsp black cumin seeds
4 green chillies
fresh coriander (cilantro) leaves, finely chopped
4 tbsp lemon juice

1 Blend together the ginger, garlic, garam masala, chilli powder, turmeric, 1 tsp salt and cardamom seeds and mix with the yogurt and chicken pieces. Set aside to marinate for 3 hours.

2 Boil the milk in a pan, pour over the saffron and set aside.

3 Heat the ghee in a pan and fry the onions until golden brown. Remove half of the onions and ghee from the saucepan and set aside.

4 Place the rice in a pan with twice as much water as rice. Add the cinnamon, peppercorns and the cumin. Bring to the boil and remove from the heat when half-cooked. Drain and place in a bowl. Mix with the remaining salt.

5 Using a sharp knife, finely chop the green chillies.

6 Add the chicken mixture to the pan containing the onions and ghee. Add half each of the chopped green chillies, coriander (cilantro), lemon juice and saffron. Add the rice and then the rest of the ingredients, including the fried onions and ghee. Cover tightly so no steam escapes. Cook on a low heat for about 1 hour. If the meat is not cooked through, cook for a further 15 minutes. Mix well before serving.

Tomato Rice

Rice cooked with tomatoes and onions will add colour to your table, especially when garnished with green chillies, coriander (cilantro) leaves and hard-boiled (hard-cooked) eggs.

Serves 4

INGREDIENTS

150 ml/^{1}/$_4$ pint/^{2}/$_3$ cup oil
2 medium onions, sliced
1 tsp onion seeds
1 tsp fresh ginger root, finely
   chopped
1 tsp fresh garlic, crushed

^{1}/$_2$ tsp turmeric
1 tsp chilli powder
1^1/$_2$ tsp salt
400 g/14 oz can tomatoes
450 g/1 lb/2^1/$_4$ cups basmati rice
600 ml/1 pint/2^1/$_2$ cups water

TO GARNISH:
3 fresh green chillies, finely chopped
fresh coriander (cilantro) leaves,
   chopped
3 hard-boiled (hard-cooked) eggs

1 Heat the oil in a saucepan and fry the onions until golden brown.

2 Add the onion seeds, ginger, garlic, turmeric, chilli powder and salt, stirring to combine.

3 Reduce the heat, add the tomatoes and stir-fry for 10 minutes, breaking up the tomatoes.

4 Add the rice to the tomato mixture, stirring gently, to coat the rice in the mixture.

5 Pour in the water, stirring to incorporate. Cover the pan and cook over a low heat until the water has been absorbed and the rice is cooked.

6 Transfer the tomato rice to a serving dish.

7 Garnish the tomato rice with the finely chopped green chillies, fresh coriander (cilantro) leaves and hard-boiled (hard-cooked) eggs. Serve the tomato rice immediately.

COOK'S TIP

Onion seeds are always used whole in Indian cooking. They are often used in pickles and often sprinkled over the top of Naan Breads (see page 178). Ironically, onion seeds don't have anything to do with the vegetable, but they look similar to the plant's seed, hence the name.

Lamb Biryani

Cooked on festive occasions, especially for weddings, lamb biryani *is amongst the most popular dishes in India. The meat can be cooked in advance and added to the rice on the day of the party.*

Serves 4–6

INGREDIENTS

150 ml/¹/₄ pint/²/₃ cup milk
1 tsp saffron
5 tbsp ghee
3 medium onions, sliced
1 kg/2 lb 5 oz lean lamb, cubed
7 tbsp natural yogurt
1¹/₂ tsp fresh ginger root, finely
   chopped

1¹/₂ tsp fresh garlic, crushed
2 tsp garam masala
2 tsp salt
¹/₄ tsp turmeric
600 ml/1 pint/2¹/₂ cups water
450 g/1 lb/2¹/₄ cups basmati rice
2 tsp black cumin seeds
3 cardamoms

4 tbsp lemon juice
2 fresh green chillies
¹/₄ bunch fresh coriander (cilantro)
   leaves

1 Boil the milk in a pan with the saffron and set aside. Heat the ghee in a pan and fry the onions until golden. Remove half of the onions and ghee from the pan and set aside in a bowl.

2 Combine the meat, yogurt, ginger, garlic, garam masala, 1 tsp salt and turmeric in a large bowl and mix well.

3 Return the pan with the ghee and onions to the heat, add the meat mixture, stir for about 3 minutes and add the water. Cook over a low heat for 45 minutes, stirring occasionally. Check to see whether the meat is tender: if not, add 150 ml/¹/₄ pint/²/₃ cup water and cook for 15 minutes. Once all the water has evaporated, stir-fry for about 2 minutes and set aside.

4 Meanwhile, place the rice in a pan. Add the cumin seeds, cardamoms, salt and enough water for cooking, and cook over a medium heat until the rice is half-cooked. Drain. Remove half of the rice and place in a bowl.

5 Spoon the meat mixture on top of the rice in the pan. Add half each of the saffron mixture, lemon juice, chillies and coriander (cilantro). Add the reserved onion and ghee mixture, the other half of the rice, saffron, lemon juice, chillies and coriander (cilantro). Cover and cook over a low heat for 15-20 minutes. Serve hot.

Paratas stuffed with Vegetables

This bread can be quite rich and is usually made for special occasions.
It can be eaten on its own or with any meat or vegetable curry.

Makes 4–6

INGREDIENTS

DOUGH:
225 g/8 oz/1³/₄ cups wholemeal flour
   (*ata* or *chapati* flour)
¹/₂ tsp salt
200 ml/¹/₃ pint/³/₄ cup water
100 g/3¹/₂ oz/8 tbsp pure or
   vegetable ghee

2 tbsp ghee, for frying

FILLING:
3 medium potatoes
¹/₂ tsp turmeric
1 tsp garam masala

1 tsp fresh ginger root, finely
   chopped
fresh coriander (cilantro) leaves
3 green chillies, finely chopped
1 tsp salt

1 To make the *paratas*, mix the flour, salt, water and ghee in a bowl to form a dough.

2 Divide the dough into 6-8 equal portions. Roll each portion out on to a floured work surface. Brush the middle of the dough portions with ¹/₂ tsp ghee. Fold the dough portions in half, roll into a pipe-like shape, flatten with the palms of your hand, then roll around your finger to form a coil. Roll out again, using flour to dust as and when necessary, to form a round about 18 cm/ 7 inches in diameter.

3 Place the potatoes in a saucepan of water and cook until soft enough to be mashed.

4 Blend the turmeric, garam masala, ginger, coriander (cilantro), chillies and salt together in a bowl.

5 Add the spice mixture to the mashed potato and mix well. Spread about 1 tbsp of the spicy potato mixture on each dough portion and cover with another rolled-out piece of dough. Seal the edges well.

6 Heat 2 tsp ghee in a heavy-bottomed frying-pan (skillet). Place the *paratas* gently in the pan in batches and fry, turning and moving them about gently with a flat spoon, until golden.

7 Remove the *paratas* from the frying pan (skillet) and serve immediately.

Gram Flour Bread

This filling bread is not eaten on a regular basis but is cooked occasionally. It is best served with White Radish Curry (see page 110), but goes well with any vegetarian curry and lime pickle.

Makes 4–6

INGREDIENTS

100 g/3¹/2 oz/³/4 cup wholemeal flour (*ata* or *chapati* flour)
75 g/2³/4 oz/¹/2 cup gram flour

¹/2 tsp salt
1 small onion
fresh coriander (cilantro) leaves, chopped very finely

2 fresh green chillies, chopped very finely
150 ml/¹/4 pint/²/3 cup water
2 tsp ghee

1 Sift the wholemeal and gram flours together in a large mixing bowl.

2 Add the salt to the flour and mix to combine.

3 Using a sharp knife, chop the onion very finely.

4 Blend the onion, coriander (cilantro) and chillies into the flour mixture.

5 Add the water and mix to form a soft dough. Cover the dough and set aside for about 15 minutes.

6 Knead the dough for 5-7 minutes.

7 Divide the dough into 8 equal portions.

8 Roll out the dough portions to about 18 cm/7 inches on a lightly floured surface.

9 Place the dough portions individually in a frying-pan (skillet) and cook over a medium heat, turning three times and lightly greasing each side with the ghee each time. Transfer the gram flour bread to serving plates and serve hot.

COOK'S TIP

Also called besan flour, gram flour is a pale yellow flour made from ground chick-peas (garbanzo beans). In Indian kitchens it is used to make breads, bhajis and batters and to thicken sauces and stabilize yogurt when it is added to hot dishes. Buy it from Indian food stores or large health food stores and store in a cool, dark place in an air-tight container.

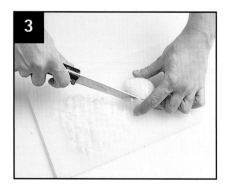

Naan Bread

There are many ways of making naan bread, but this particular recipe is very easy to follow. Naan bread should be served warm, preferably immediately after cooking.

Makes 6-8

INGREDIENTS

1 tsp sugar
1 tsp fresh yeast
150 ml/^{1}/4 pint/^{2}/3 cup warm water

200 g/7 oz/1^1/2 cups plain (all-purpose) flour
1 tbsp ghee

1 tsp salt
50 g/1^3/4 oz/6 tbsp unsalted butter
1 tsp poppy seeds

1 Put the sugar and yeast in a small bowl or jug with the warm water and mix well until the yeast has dissolved. Set aside for about 10 minutes or until the mixture is frothy.

2 Place the flour in a large mixing bowl. Make a well in the middle of the flour, add the ghee and salt and pour in the yeast mixture. Mix well to form a dough, using your hands and adding more water if required.

3 Turn the dough out on to a floured surface and knead for about 5 minutes or until smooth.

4 Return the dough to the bowl, cover and leave to rise in a warm place for 1½ hours or until doubled in size.

5 Turn the dough out on to a floured surface and knead for a further 2 minutes. Break off small balls with your hand and pat them into rounds about 12 cm/ 5 inches in diameter and 1 cm/ ½ inch thick.

6 Place the dough rounds on to a greased sheet of foil and grill (broil) under a very hot pre-heated grill (broiler) for 7-10 minutes, turning twice and brushing with

the butter and sprinkling with the poppy seeds.

7 Serve warm immediately, or keep wrapped in foil until required.

COOK'S TIP

A tandoor oven throws out a ferocious heat; this bread is traditionally cooked on the side wall of the oven where the heat is only slightly less than in the centre. For an authentic effect, leave your grill (broiler) on for a long time to heat up before the first dough goes under.

Poori

This bread is served mostly with vegetarian meals and particularly with Potato Curry (see page 116) and Semolina Dessert (see page 244). Although pooris *are deep-fried, they are very light.*

Makes 10

INGREDIENTS

225 g/8 oz/1^1/2 cups wholemeal flour (*ata* or *chapati* flour)

^{1}/2 tsp salt
150 ml/^{1}/4 pint/^{2}/3 cup water

600 ml/1 pint/2^1/2 cups oil

1 Place the flour and salt in a large mixing bowl and stir to combine.

2 Make a well in the centre of the flour. Gradually pour in the water and mix together to form a dough, adding more water if necessary.

3 Knead the dough until it is smooth and elastic and set aside in a warm place to rise for about 15 minutes.

4 Divide the dough into about 10 equal portions and with lightly oiled or floured hands pat each into a smooth ball.

5 On a lightly oiled or floured surface, roll out each ball to form a thin round.

6 Heat the oil in a deep frying-pan (skillet). Deep-fry the rounds in batches, turning once, until golden in colour.

7 Remove the *pooris* from the pan and drain. Serve hot.

COOK'S TIP

You can serve pooris *either piled one on top of the other or spread out in a layer on a large serving platter so that they remain puffed up.*

COOK'S TIP

You can make pooris *in advance, if you prefer. Wrap in kitchen foil and reheat in a hot oven for about 10 minutes when required.*

Snacks & Side Dishes

In India, we like having tea parties at about 5 or 6 o'clock in the evening, especially in the month of Ramadan, when people meet after fasting all day, and we serve little snacks such as the ones in this chapter. They are ideal for cocktail or other drinks parties, when you would like to offer something more interesting than the usual peanuts and crisps. The basic quantities are for 4 people, but you can multiply according to the number on your guest list.

Accompaniments – a simple Carrot Salad or a Mint Raita, for example – always add colour and variety to a meal. Most take very little time to prepare, but taste delicious. None of these accompaniments has to be made in large quantities, because they are only taken in small amounts: variety is better than quantity!

Fried Aubergines (Eggplants) in Yogurt

*This makes a good alternative to a Raita (see page 216). The aubergines (eggplants)
are fried until crisp, then given a* baghaar, *or seasoned oil dressing.*

Serves 4

INGREDIENTS

200 ml/7 fl oz/³/₄ cup natural yogurt
75 ml/3 fl oz/¹/₃ cup water
1 tsp salt

1 medium aubergine (eggplant)
150 ml/¹/₄ pint/²/₃ cup oil
1 tsp white cumin seeds

6 dried red chillies

1 Place the yogurt in a bowl and whip with a fork.

2 Add the water and salt to the yogurt and mix well. Transfer to a serving bowl.

3 Using a sharp knife, slice the aubergine (eggplant) thinly.

4 Heat the oil in a large frying-pan (skillet). Add the aubergine (eggplant) slices and fry, in batches, over a medium heat, turning occasionally, until they begin to turn crisp. Remove from the pan, transfer to a serving plate and keep warm.

5 When all of the aubergine (eggplant) slices have been fried, lower the heat, and add the white cumin seeds and the dried red chillies to the pan. Cook for 1 minute, stirring.

6 Spoon the yogurt on top of the aubergines (eggplants), then pour over the white cumin and red chilli mixture. Serve immediately.

VARIATION

*Finely chop and deseed the dried
red chillies, if you prefer.*

COOK'S TIP

*Rich in protein and calcium, yogurt
plays an important part in Indian
cooking. It is used as a marinade,
as a creamy flavouring in curries
and sauces and as a cooling
accompaniment to hot dishes.*

Spicy Corn

This dish is an ideal accompaniment to a wide range of Indian meals.

Serves 4

INGREDIENTS

200 g/7 oz/1 cup canned or frozen
  sweetcorn
1 tsp ground cumin
1 tsp fresh garlic, crushed

1 tsp ground coriander
1 tsp salt
2 fresh green chillies
1 medium onion, finely chopped

3 tbsp unsalted butter
4 red chillies, crushed
$^1/_2$ tsp lemon juice
fresh coriander (cilantro) leaves

1 Thaw or drain the sweetcorn (if using canned sweetcorn) and set aside.

2 Place the ground cumin, garlic, ground coriander, salt, 1 fresh green chilli and the onion in a pestle and mortar or a food processor and grind to form a smooth paste.

3 Heat the butter in a large frying pan (skillet). Add the onion and spice mixture to the pan and fry over a medium heat, stirring occasionally, for about 5-7 minutes.

4 Add the crushed red chillies to the pan and stir to mix.

5 Add the sweetcorn to the pan and stir-fry for a further 2 minutes.

6 Add the remaining green chilli, lemon juice and the fresh coriander (cilantro) leaves to the pan, stirring occasionally to combine.

7 Transfer the spicy sweetcorn mixture to a warm serving dish. Garnish with fresh coriander (cilantro) and serve hot.

COOK'S TIP

Coriander is available ground or as seeds and is one of the essential ingredients in Indian cooking. Coriander seeds are often dry roasted before use to develop their flavour.

Pakoras

Pakoras are eaten all over India. They are made in many different ways and with a variety of fillings. Sometimes they are served in yogurt.

Serves 4

INGREDIENTS

6 tbsp gram flour
$^1/_2$ tsp salt
1 tsp chilli powder
1 tsp baking powder
$1^1/_2$ tsp white cumin seeds

1 tsp pomegranate seeds
300 ml/$^1/_2$ pint/$1^1/_4$ cups water
fresh coriander (cilantro) leaves, finely chopped

vegetables of your choice:
    cauliflower, cut into small florets, onions, cut into rings, potatoes, sliced, aubergines (eggplants), sliced, or fresh spinach leaves)
oil, for deep-frying

1 Sift the gram flour into a large mixing bowl.

2 Add the salt, chilli powder, baking powder, cumin and pomegranate seeds and blend together well.

3 Pour in the water and beat well to form a smooth batter.

4 Add the coriander (cilantro) and mix. Set the batter aside.

5 Dip the prepared vegetables of your choice into the batter, carefully shaking off any of the excess batter.

6 Heat the oil in a large heavy-based pan. Place the battered vegetables of your choice in the oil and deep-fry, in batches, turning once.

7 Repeat this process until all of the batter has been used up.

8 Transfer the battered vegetables to kitchen paper and drain thoroughly. Serve immediately.

COOK'S TIP

When deep-frying, it is important to use oil at the correct temperature. If the oil is too hot, the outside of the food will burn as will the spices, before the inside is cooked. If the oil is too cool, the food will be sodden with oil before a crisp batter forms. Draining on kitchen paper is essential as it absorbs excess oil and moisture.

Indian-Style Omelette

I find omelettes very versatile: they go with almost anything and you can also serve them at any time of the day. For an informal lunch you could serve this omelette with chips (fries).

Serves 2–4

INGREDIENTS

1 small onion, very finely chopped
2 green chillies, finely chopped

fresh coriander (cilantro) leaves, finely chopped

4 medium eggs
1 tsp salt
2 tbsp oil

1 Place the onion, chillies and coriander (cilantro) in a large mixing bowl. Mix together, ideally with your fingers.

2 Place the eggs in a separate bowl and whisk together.

3 Add the onion mixture to the eggs and mix together.

4 Add the salt to the egg and onion mixture and whisk together well.

5 Heat 1 tbsp of the oil in a large frying pan (skillet). Place a ladleful of the omelette batter into the pan.

6 Fry the omelette, turning once and pressing down with a flat spoon to make sure that the egg is cooked right through, until the omelette is a golden brown colour.

7 Repeat the same process for the remaining batter. Set the omelettes aside and keep warm while you make the remaining batches of omelettes.

8 Serve the omelettes immediately with Paratas (see page 174) or toasted bread. Alternatively, simply serve the omelettes with a crisp green salad for a light lunch.

COOK'S TIP

Indian cooks use a variety of vegetable oils, and groundnut or sunflower oils make good alternatives for most dishes, although sometimes more specialist ones, such as coconut oil, mustard oil and sesame oil, are called for.

Samosas

Samosas, which are a sort of Indian Cornish pasty, make excellent snacks. In India you can buy them along the roadside, and they are very popular. They are may be frozen and re-heated.

Makes 10–12

INGREDIENTS

PASTRY:
100 g/3^1/2 oz/^{3}/4 cup self-raising
   flour
^{1}/2 tsp salt
40 g/1^1/2 oz/3 tbsp butter, cut into
   small pieces
4 tbsp water

FILLING:
3 medium potatoes, boiled
1 tsp fresh ginger root, finely
   chopped
1 tsp fresh garlic, crushed
^{1}/2 tsp white cumin seeds
^{1}/2 tsp mixed onion and mustard
   seeds

1 tsp salt
^{1}/2 tsp crushed red chillies
2 tbsp lemon juice
2 small green chillies, finely chopped
ghee or oil, for deep-frying

1 Sift the flour and salt into a large mixing bowl. Add the butter and rub into the flour until the mixture resembles fine breadcrumbs.

2 Pour in the water and mix with a fork to form a dough. Pat the dough into a ball and knead for 5 minutes or until the dough is smooth. Add a little flour if the dough is sticky. Cover and leave to rise.

3 To make the filling, mash the boiled potatoes gently and mix with the ginger, garlic, white cumin seeds, onion and mustard seeds, salt, crushed red chillies, lemon juice and green chilli.

4 Break small balls off the dough and roll each out very thinly to form a round. Cut in half, dampen the edges and shape into cones. Fill the cones with a little of the filling, dampen the top

and bottom edges of the cones and pinch together to seal Set aside.

5 Fill a deep pan one-third full with oil and heat to 180°-190°C/350°-375°F or until a small cube of bread browns in 30 seconds. Carefully lower the samosas into the oil, a few at a time, and fry for 2-3 minutes or until golden brown. Remove from the oil and drain thoroughly on kitchen towels. Serve hot or cold.

Soft Dumplings in Yogurt with Masala

These are very light and make a good summer afternoon snack as well as a good accompaniment to any vegetarian meal. They are usually served with their own special spice mixture in a small dish.

Serves 4

INGREDIENTS

200 g/7 oz/1^{1}/$_{2}$ cups *urid dhaal* powder
1 tsp baking powder
^{1}/$_{2}$ tsp ground ginger
300 ml/^{1}/$_{2}$ pint/1^{1}/$_{4}$ cups water
oil, for deep-frying

400 ml/14 fl oz/1^{1}/$_{2}$ cups natural yogurt
75 g/2^{3}/$_{4}$ oz/5 tbsp sugar

MASALA:
50 g/1^{3}/$_{4}$ oz/6 tbsp ground coriander

50 g/1^{3}/$_{4}$ oz/6 tbsp ground white cumin
25 g/1 oz crushed red chillies
100 g/3^{1}/$_{2}$ oz/^{1}/$_{2}$ cup citric acid
chopped red chillies, to garnish

1 Place the powdered *urid dhaal* in a large mixing bowl. Add the baking powder and ginger powder and stir to combine. Add the water and mix to form a paste.

2 Heat the oil in a deep pan or frying pan (skillet). Pour in the batter, 1 tsp at a time, and deep-fry the dumplings until golden brown, lowering the heat when the oil gets too hot. Set the dumplings aside.

3 Place the yogurt in a separate bowl. Add 400 ml/15 fl oz/1^{3}/$_{4}$ cups water and the sugar and mix together with a whisk or fork. Set aside.

4 To make the *masala*, roast the ground coriander and the white cumin in a saucepan until a little darker in colour. Grind coarsely in a food processor or pestle and mortar. Add the crushed red chillies and citric acid and blend well together.

5 Sprinkle about 1 tbsp of the *masala* over the dumplings and garnish with chopped red chillies. Serve with the reserved yogurt mixture.

COOK'S TIP

The masala *(spice mixture) for the dumplings is usually made in a large quantity as it can be stored in an airtight container.*

Spiced Semolina

A south Indian savoury snack which is very quick and easy to prepare, this should be served warm. It has a lovely aroma, mainly from the curry leaves.

Serves 4

INGREDIENTS

150 ml/¼ pint/⅔ cup oil
1 tsp mixed onion and mustard seeds
4 dried red chillies

4 curry leaves (fresh or dried)
8 tbsp coarse semolina
50 g/1¾ oz cashew nuts

1 tsp salt
150 ml/¼ pint/⅔ cup water

1 Heat the oil in a large, heavy frying-pan (skillet).

2 Add the mixed onion and mustard seeds, dried red chillies and curry leaves and stir-fry for about 1 minute, stirring constantly.

3 Reduce the heat and add the coarse semolina and the cashew nuts to the mixture in the pan. Quickly stir-fry for about 5 minutes, moving the mixture around the pan all the time so that it does not catch and burn on the bottom of the pan.

4 Add the salt to the mixture and continue to stir-fry, stirring constantly.

5 Add the water and cook, stirring continuously, until the mixture starts to thicken.

6 Serve the spiced semolina warm as a teatime snack.

COOK'S TIP

The basic quantity here is for 4 people, which you can multiply according to your guest list.

COOK'S TIP

Curry leaves are very similar in appearance to bay leaves but are very different in flavour. They can be bought both fresh and dried. They are mainly used to flavour lentil dishes and vegetable curries.

Sweet & Sour Fruit

This mixture of fresh and canned fruit, which has a sweet and sour flavour,
is very cooling, especially in the summer. We would serve tea or fruit juices with this.

Serves 4

INGREDIENTS

400 g/14 oz can mixed fruit cocktail
400 g/14 oz can guavas
2 large bananas

3 apples
1 tsp ground black pepper
1 tsp salt

2 tbsp lemon juice
1/2 tsp ground ginger
fresh mint leaves, to garnish

1 Drain the fruit cocktail and place the fruit in a deep mixing bowl.

2 Mix the guavas and their syrup with the drained fruit cocktail.

3 Peel the bananas and cut into slices.

4 Peel the apples (optional) and cut into dice.

5 Add the fresh fruit to the bowl containing the canned fruit and mix together.

6 Add the ground black pepper, salt, lemon juice and ginger and stir to mix.

7 Serve as a snack garnished with a few fresh mint leaves.

COOK'S TIP

The lemon juice in this recipe serves to add a sharp flavour to the dish but it also prevents the banana and apple from dicolouring and turning brown when the flesh is exposed to the air.

COOK'S TIP

Ginger is one of the most popular spices in India and also one of the oldest. It can be bought as fresh ginger root in most large supermarkets. It should always be peeled before use and can be finely chopped or puréed. Ground ginger is also useful to have in your storecupboard.

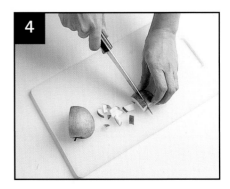

Mixed Rice, Nuts & Raisins

This is one of the most popular nut mixtures in India and is very tasty. I recommend that you make a large quantity and store it in an airtight container to serve with tea or alcoholic drinks.

Serves 4

INGREDIENTS

50 g/1³/4 oz/¹/3 cup *chana dhaal*
300 ml/¹/2 pint/1¹/4 cups oil
2 tsp onion seeds
6 curry leaves

200 g/7 oz/3 cups *parva* (flaked rice)
2 tbsp peanuts
25 g/1 oz/2 tbsp raisins
75 g/2³/4 oz/5 tbsp sugar

2 tsp salt
2 tsp chilli powder
50 g/2 oz *sev* (optional)

1 Rinse and soak the *chana dhaal* in a bowl of water for at least 3 hours.

2 Heat the oil in a saucepan. Add the onion seeds and the curry leaves and fry, stirring constantly, until the onion seeds are crisp and golden.

3 Add the *parva* (flaked rice) to the mixture in the pan and fry until crisp and golden (do not allow to burn).

4 Remove the mixture from the pan and leave to drain on paper towels so that any excess oil is soaked up.

5 Fry the peanuts in the remaining oil, stirring.

6 Add the peanuts to the flaked rice mixture, stirring to mix well.

7 Add the raisins, sugar, salt and chilli powder and mix together. Mix in the *sev* (if using). Transfer to a serving dish.

8 Re-heat the oil remaining in the pan and fry the soaked *chana dhaal* until golden. Add to the other ingredients in the serving dish and mix together.

9 This dish can be eaten straight away or stored in an airtight container until you need it.

COOK'S TIP

Sev are very thin sticks made of gram flour which can be bought in Indian and Pakistani grocers.

Deep-Fried Diamond Pastries

A simple-to-make snack which will retain its crispness if stored in an airtight container. Serve with drinks or at tea-time.

Serves 4

INGREDIENTS

150 g/5^1/$_2$ oz/1 cup plain (all-purpose) flour
1 tsp baking powder

^{1}/$_2$ tsp salt
1 tbsp black cumin seeds
100 ml/3^1/$_2$ fl oz/^{1}/$_2$ cup water

300 ml/^{1}/$_2$ pint/1^1/$_4$ cups oil

1 Place the flour in a large mixing bowl.

2 Add the baking powder, salt and the black cumin seeds and stir to mix.

3 Add the water to the dry ingredients and mix to form a soft, elasticated dough.

4 Roll out the dough on to a clean work surface (counter) until about 6 mm/^{1}/$_4$ inch thick.

5 Using a sharp knife, score the dough to form diamond shapes. Re-roll the dough and cut out more diamond shapes until all of the dough has been used up.

6 Heat the oil in a large pan to 180°-190°C/350°-375°F or until a cube of bread browns in 30 seconds.

7 Carefully place the pastry diamonds in the oil, in batches if necessary, and deep-fry until golden brown.

8 Remove the diamond pastries with a perforated spoon and leave to drain on paper towels. Serve with a *dhaal* for dipping or store and serve when required.

COOK'S TIP

Black cumin seeds are used here for their strong aromatic flavour. White cumin seeds may not be used as a substitute.

Hot Salad

This quickly-made dish is ideal for a cold winter's night.

Serves 4

INGREDIENTS

¹/₂ medium-sized cauliflower	¹/₂ cucumber	salt and pepper
1 green (bell) pepper	4 carrots	
1 red (bell) pepper	2 tbsp butter	

1 Rinse the cauliflower and cut into small florets, using a sharp knife.

2 Cut the (bell) peppers into thin slices.

3 Cut the cucumber into thin slices.

4 Peel the carrots and cut them into thin slices.

5 Melt the butter in a large saucepan, stirring constantly so that it doesn't burn.

6 Add the cauliflower, (bell) peppers, cucumber and carrots and stir-fry for 5-7 minutes. Season with salt and pepper to taste, cover with a lid, reduce the heat and leave to simmer for about 3 minutes.

7 Transfer the vegetables to a serving dish, toss to mix, and serve immediately.

COOK'S TIP

In India, you can buy snacks and accompaniments along the roadside while elsewhere you can either buy them from Indian or Pakistani grocers. However, they are fresher and more satisfying made at home.

VARIATION

You can replace the vegetables in this recipe with those of your choice, if you prefer.

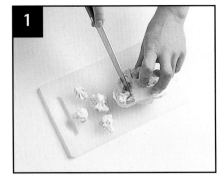

Cool Cucumber Salad

This cooling salad is another good foil for a highly spiced meal.
Omit the green chilli, if preferred.

Serves 4

INGREDIENTS

225 g/8 oz cucumber
1 green chilli (optional)

fresh coriander (cilantro) leaves,
   finely chopped
2 tbsp lemon juice

¹/₂ tsp salt
1 tsp sugar
fresh mint leaves, to garnish

1 Using a sharp knife, slice the cucumber thinly. Arrange the cucumber slices on a round serving plate.

2 Using a sharp knife, chop the green chilli (if using).

3 Scatter the chopped chilli over the cucumber.

4 To make the dressing, place the coriander (cilantro), lemon juice, salt and sugar into a bowl, mix together and set aside.

5 Place the cucumber in the refrigerator and leave to chill for at least 1 hour, or until required.

6 Transfer the cucumber to a serving dish.

7 Pour the dressing over the cucumber just before serving and garnish with a few fresh mint leaves.

COOK'S TIP

To store fresh coriander (cilantro), put the roots in a glass of water and keep in a cool place for up to 4 days.

COOK'S TIP

Much of the heat in Indian dishes comes from the use of fresh green chillies, although dried and ground red chillies are also commonplace in Indian kitchens. In southern India, with it's searingly hot temperatures, chillies are used in copious amounts because they cause the body to perspire, which has a cooling effect. Numerous varieties of fresh chilli grow in India, from fairly mild to hot. As a general rule, the smaller the chilli, the hotter it will be. Fresh chillies will keep for about 5 days in the refrigerator.

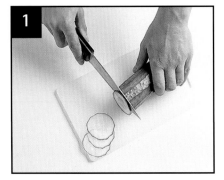

Chick-Pea (Garbanzo Bean) Salad

This attractive-looking salad can be served with a couple of Beef Kebabs (Kabobs) (see page 46) for a delicious light lunch or an informal supper.

Serves 4

INGREDIENTS

400 g/14 oz can chick-peas (garbanzo beans)	1 medium cucumber	1 red (bell) pepper, sliced
4 carrots	1/2 tsp salt	
1 bunch spring onions (scallions)	1/2 tsp pepper	
	3 tbsp lemon juice	

1 Drain the chick-peas (garbanzo beans) and place them in a large salad bowl.

2 Using a sharp knife, peel and slice the carrots.

3 Cut the spring onions (scallions) into small pieces.

4 Cut the cucumber into thick quarters.

5 Add the carrots, spring onions (scallions) and cucumber to the chick-peas (garbanzo beans) and mix.

6 Season with the salt and pepper and sprinkle with the lemon juice.

7 Toss the salad ingredients together gently using 2 serving spoons.

8 Using a sharp knife, slice the red (bell) pepper thinly.

9 Arrange the slices of red (bell) pepper on top of the chick-pea (garbanzo bean) salad. Serve the salad immediately or leave to chill in the refrigerator and serve when required.

COOK'S TIP

Using canned chick-peas (garbanzo beans) rather than the dried ones speeds up the cooking time.

Raitas

*Raitas are very easy to prepare, very versatile and have a cooling effect
which will be appreciated if you are serving hot, spicy dishes.*

Serves 4

INGREDIENTS

MINT RAITA:

200 ml/7 fl oz/³/₄ cup natural yogurt
50 ml/2 fl oz/4 tbsp water
1 small onion, finely chopped
¹/₂ tsp mint sauce
¹/₂ tsp salt
3 fresh mint leaves, to garnish

CUCUMER RAITA:

225 g/8 oz cucumber
1 medium onion
¹/₂ tsp salt
¹/₂ tsp mint sauce
300 ml/10 fl oz/1¹/₄ cups yogurt
150 ml/¹/₄ pint/²/₃ cup water
fresh mint leaves, to garnish

AUBERGINE (EGGPLANT) RAITA:

1 medium aubergine (eggplant)
1 tsp salt
1 small onion, finely chopped
2 green chillies, finely chopped
200 ml/7 fl oz/³/₄ cup natural yogurt
3 tbsp water

1 To make the mint raita, place the yogurt in a bowl and whisk with a fork. Gradually add the water, whisking well. Add the onion, mint sauce and salt and blend together. Garnish with the fresh mint leaves.

2 To make the cucumber raita, peel and slice the cucumber. Using a sharp knife, chop the onion finely. Place the cucumber and onion in a large bowl, then add the salt and the mint sauce. Add the yogurt and the water and place the mixture in a liquidizer and blend well. Transfer to a serving bowl and serve garnished with a few fresh mint leaves.

3 To make the aubergine (eggplant) raita, rinse the aubergine (eggplant) and remove the top end. Discard the top and chop the rest into small pieces. Boil the aubergine (eggplant) in a pan of water until soft and mushy. Drain the aubergine (eggplant) and mash. Transfer to a serving bowl and add the salt, the onion and green chillies, mixing well. Whip the yogurt with the water in a separate bowl and pour over the aubergine (eggplant) mixture. Mix well and serve.

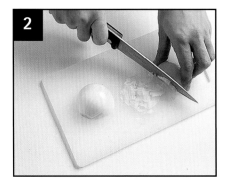

Mango Chutney

Everyone's favourite chutney, this has a sweet and sour taste and is particularly good served with a Mint Raita (see page 216). It is best made well in advance and stored for at least 2 weeks before use.

Serves 4

INGREDIENTS

1 kg/2 lb 4 oz raw mangoes
4 tbsp salt
600 ml/1 pint/2^{1}/$_{2}$ cups water
450 g/1 lb/2^{1}/$_{3}$ cups sugar
450 ml/^{3}/$_{4}$ pint/2 cups vinegar

2 tsp fresh ginger root, finely chopped
2 tsp fresh garlic, crushed
2 tsp chilli powder
2 cinnamon sticks

75 g/2^{3}/$_{4}$ oz/^{1}/$_{2}$ cup raisins
100 g/3^{1}/$_{2}$ oz/^{1}/$_{2}$ cup dates, stoned

1 Using a sharp knife, peel, halve and stone the mangoes. Cut the mango flesh into cubes. Place the mango in a large bowl. Add the salt and water and leave overnight. Drain the liquid from the mangoes and set aside.

2 Bring the sugar and vinegar to the boil in a large saucepan over a low heat, stirring.

3 Gradually add the mango cubes to the sugar and vinegar mixture, stirring to coat the mango in the mixture.

4 Add the ginger, garlic, chilli powder, cinnamon sticks, raisins and the dates, and bring to the boil again, stirring occasionally. Reduce the heat and cook for about 1 hour or until the mixture thickens. Remove from the heat and leave to cool.

5 Remove the cinnamon sticks and discard.

6 Spoon the chutney into clean dry jars and cover tightly with lids. Leave in a cool place for the flavours to fully develop.

COOK'S TIP

When choosing mangoes, select ones that are shiny with unblemished skins. To test if they are ripe, gently cup the mango in your hand and squeeze it gently – it should give slightly to the touch if ready for eating.

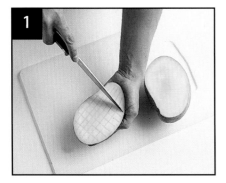

Seasame Seed Chutney

This chutney was always served with Spiced Rice & Lentils (see page 154) in our house in India, and the combination still appeals to me. I also use it to spread in sandwiches.

Serves 4

INGREDIENTS

8 tbsp sesame seeds
2 tbsp water
1/2 bunch fresh coriander (cilantro)

3 fresh green chillies, chopped
1 tsp salt
2 tsp lemon juice

chopped red chilli, to garnish

1 Place the sesame seeds in a large, heavy-based saucepan and dry roast them.

2 Set the sesame seeds aside to cool.

3 Once cooled, place the sesame seeds in a food processor or pestle and mortar and grind to form a fine powder.

4 Add the water to the sesame seeds and mix to form a smooth paste.

5 Using a sharp knife, finely chop the coriander (cilantro).

6 Add the chillies and coriander (cilantro) to the sesame seed paste and grind once again.

7 Add the salt and lemon juice to the mixture and grind once again.

8 Remove the mixture from the food processor or pestle and mortar and transfer to a serving dish. Garnish and serve.

COOK'S TIP

Rinsing raw onions with water takes the edge off the raw taste.

COOK'S TIP

Dry roasting coaxes all of the flavour out of dried spices and gives dishes well-harmonized flavours that do not taste raw. Dry roasting only takes a few minutes and you will be able to tell when the spices are ready because of the wonderful fragrance that develops. Be sure to stir the spices constantly and never take your eyes off the pan because the spices can burn very quickly.

Tamarind Chutney

A mouth-watering chutney which is extremely popular all over India, served with various vegetarian snacks. I enjoy this particularly with Samosas (see page 196).

Serves 4-6

INGREDIENTS

2 tbsp tamarind paste
5 tbsp water
1 tsp chilli powder

$^{1}/_{2}$ tsp ground ginger
$^{1}/_{2}$ tsp salt
1 tsp sugar

finely chopped coriander (cilantro) leaves, to garnish

1 Place the tamarind paste into a mixing bowl.

2 Gradually add the water to the tamarind paste, gently whisking with a fork to form a smooth, runny paste.

3 Add the chilli powder and the ginger to the mixture and blend well.

4 Add the salt and the sugar and mix well.

5 Transfer the chutney to a serving dish and garnish with the coriander (cilantro).

COOK'S TIP

Vegetable dishes are often given a sharp, sour flavour with the addition of tamarind. This is made from the semi-dried, compressed pulp of the tamarind tree. You can buy bars of the pungent-smelling pulp in Indian and oriental grocery stores. Store it in a tightly sealed plastic bag or airtight container. Alternatively, for greater convenience, keep a jar of tamarind paste in your storecupboard and use as required. Although tamarind is much stronger than lemon, lemon is often used as a substitute.

COOK'S TIP

Chilli powder, or cayenne pepper, is a very fiery spice that should be used with caution.

Desserts

Indian meals, usually end with something sweet, just as they do in the West. Indian desserts are quite rich and very sweet, so it is a good idea to offer a choice of fresh fruit – mangoes, guavas or melon, for example – as well. These are best served chilled, especially in the summer months.

Among Indian people, desserts such as Indian Bread Pudding, Carrot Dessert and Indian Vermicelli Dessert are served only for special occasions, such as a religious festival. In this chapter, I have also included some simple desserts such as Indian Rice Pudding as well as the more elaborate desserts. Do try some of these dishes, I find that because few restaurants offer much in the way of special Indian desserts they are usually a complete revelation to my Western guests – and always a pleasant one!

Almond Slices

A mouth-watering dessert that is sure to impress your guests,
especially if served with whipped cream

Serves 6-8

INGREDIENTS

3 medium eggs
75 g/2³/₄ oz/¹/₂ cup ground almonds
200 g/7 oz/1¹/₂ cups milk powder

200 g/7 oz/1 cup sugar
¹/₂ tsp saffron strands
100 g/3¹/₂ oz/8 tbsp unsalted butter

25 g/1 oz/1 tbsp flaked almonds

1 Beat the eggs together in a bowl and set aside.

2 Place the ground almonds, milk powder, sugar and saffron in a large mixing bowl and stir to mix well.

3 Melt the butter in a small saucepan.

4 Pour the melted butter over the dry ingredients and mix well with a fork.

5 Add the reserved beaten eggs to the mixture and stir to blend well.

6 Spread the mixture in a shallow 15-20 cm/7-9 inch ovenproof dish and bake in a preheated oven at 160°C/325°F/Gas Mark 3 for 45 minutes. Test whether the cake is cooked through by piercing with the tip of a knife or a skewer – it will come out clean if it is cooked thoroughly.

7 Cut the almond cake mixture into slices.

8 Decorate the almond slices with flaked almonds and transfer to serving plates. Serve hot or cold.

COOK'S TIP

These almond slices are best eaten hot but they may also be served cold. They can be made a day or even a week in advance and re-heated. They also freeze beautifully.

Sweet Potato Dessert

This milky dessert can be eaten hot or cold.

Serves 8–10

INGREDIENTS

1 kg/2 lb 4 oz sweet potatoes
850 ml/1^1/$_2$ pints/3^1/$_2$ cups milk

175 g/6 oz/1^3/$_4$ cups sugar

a few chopped almonds, to decorate

1 Using a sharp knife, peel the sweet potatoes. Rinse the sweet potatoes and cut them into slices.

2 Place the sweet potato slices in a large saucepan. Cover with 600 ml/1 pint/2^1/$_2$ cups milk and cook slowly until the sweet potato is soft enough to be mashed.

3 Remove the sweet potatoes from the heat and mash to remove all the lumps.

4 Add the sugar and the remaining 300 ml/^{1}/$_2$ pint/ 1^1/$_4$ cups milk to the mashed sweet potatoes, and carefully stir to blend together.

5 Return the pan to the heat and leave the mixture to simmer until it starts to thicken (it should reach the consistency of a cream of chicken soup).

6 Transfer the sweet potato dessert to a serving dish.

7 Decorate with the chopped almonds and serve.

COOK'S TIP

Sweet potatoes are longer than ordinary potatoes and have a pinkish or yellowish skin with yellow or white flesh. As their name suggests, they taste slightly sweet.

Deep-Fried Sweetmeat in Syrup

This is one of the most popular Indian sweetmeats. The flavour and beautiful aroma of this sweetmeat comes from rosewater. The finished dish can be served hot or cold.

Serves 6-8

INGREDIENTS

5 tbsp dried full-cream milk powder
1¹/₂ tbsp plain (all-purpose) flour
1 tsp baking powder
1¹/₂ tbsp unsalted butter
1 medium egg
1 tsp milk to mix (if required)

10 tbsp pure or vegetable ghee

SYRUP:
750 ml/1¹/₄ pints/3¹/₄ cups water
8 tbsp sugar
2 green cardamoms, peeled, with
    seeds crushed

1 large pinch saffron strands
2 tbsp rosewater

1 Place the dried full-cream milk powder, flour and baking powder in a bowl.

2 Place the butter in a pan and heat until melted, stirring.

3 Whisk the egg in a bowl. Add the melted butter and whisked egg to the dry ingredients and blend together with a fork (and add the 1 tsp extra milk at this stage if necessary) to form a soft dough.

4 Break the dough into about 12 small pieces and shape, in the palms of your hands, into small, smooth balls.

5 Heat the ghee in a deep frying-pan (skillet). Reduce the heat and start frying the dough balls, about 3-4 at a time, tossing and turning gently with a perforated spoon until a dark golden brown colour. Remove the sweetmeats from the pan and set aside in a deep serving bowl.

6 To make the syrup, boil the water and sugar in a pan for 7-10 minutes. Add the crushed cardamom seeds and saffron, and pour over the sweetmeats.

7 Pour the rosewater sparingly over the top. Leave to soak for about 10 minutes in order for the sweetmeats to soak up some of the syrup. Serve hot or cold.

Rice Pudding

We cook our rice pudding in a saucepan over a low heat rather than in the oven like the British version – which is also far less sweet. Rice pudding is one of the most popular of all desserts in India.

Serves 8-10

INGREDIENTS

75 g/2³/₄ oz/¹/₄ cup basmati rice
1200 ml/2 pints/5 cups milk

8 tbsp sugar

varq (silver leaf) or chopped pistachio
nuts, to decorate

1 Rinse the rice and place in a large saucepan. Add 1 pint/ 600 ml/2¹/₂ cups milk and bring to the boil over a very low heat. Cook until the milk has been completely absorbed by the rice, stirring occasionally.

2 Remove the pan from the heat. Mash the rice, making swift, round movements in the pan, for at least 5 minutes until all of the lumps have been removed.

3 Return the pan to the heat and gradually add the remaining 1 pint/600 ml/2¹/₂ cups milk. Bring to the boil over a low heat, stirring occasionally.

4 Add the sugar and continue to cook, stirring constantly, for 7-10 minutes or until the mixture is quite thick in consistency.

5 Transfer the rice pudding to a heatproof serving bowl. Decorate with *varq* (silver leaf) or chopped pistachio nuts and serve on its own or with Pooris (see page 236).

VARIATION

If you prefer, you can substitute American or Patna long-grain rice for the basmati rice, but the result won't be as good.

COOK'S TIP

Varq is edible silver that is used to decorate elaborate dishes prepared for the most special occasions and celebrations, such as weddings, in India. It is pure silver that has been beaten until it is wafer thin. It comes with a piece of backing paper which is peeled off as the varq is laid on the cooked food. It is extremely delicate and so must be handled with care. You can buy varq in Indian food stores, and remember that because it is pure silver it should be stored in an airtight bag or box so that it doesn't tarnish.

Pistachio Dessert

Rather an attractive-looking dessert, especially when decorated with varq, *this is another dish that can be prepared in advance. It is delicious served with cream.*

Serves 4–6

INGREDIENTS

850 ml/1¹/₂ pints/3¹/₂ cups water
250 g/9 oz/3 cups pistachio nuts
250 g/9 oz/1³/₄ cups full-cream
   dried milk

450 g/1 lb/2¹/₃ cups sugar
2 cardamoms, with seeds crushed
2 tbsp rosewater
a few strands saffron

TO DECORATE:
25 g/1 oz flaked almonds
fresh mint leaves

1 Boil about 1 pint/600 ml water in a saucepan. Remove the pan from the heat and soak the pistachios in this water for about 5 minutes. Drain the pistachios thoroughly and remove the skins.

2 Grind the pistachios in a food processor or pestle and mortar.

3 Add the dried milk powder to the ground pistachios and mix well.

4 To make the syrup, place the remaining 300 ml/¹/₂ pint water and the sugar in a pan and heat gently. When the liquid begins to thicken, add the cardamom seeds, rosewater and saffron.

5 Add the syrup to the pistachio mixture and cook for about 5 minutes, stirring, until the mixture thickens. Set the mixture aside and leave to cool slightly.

6 Once cooled enough to handle, roll the mixture into balls (use up all of the pistachio mixture). Decorate with the flaked almonds and fresh mint leaves and leave to set before serving.

COOK'S TIP

It is best to buy whole pistachio nuts and grind them yourself, rather than using packets of ready-ground nuts. Freshly ground nuts have the best flavour as grinding releases their natural oils.

Pooris stuffed with Chana Dhaal Halva

This is a very old recipe handed down to me by my mother. The pooris freeze well so it pays to make a large quantity and re-heat them in the oven.

Makes 10

INGREDIENTS

POORIS:
200 g/7 oz/1 cup coarse semolina
100 g/3¹/₂ oz/³/₄ cup plain (all-purpose) flour
¹/₂ tsp salt
1¹/₂ tbsp ghee, plus extra for frying

150 ml/¹/₄ pint/²/₃ cup milk

FILLING:
8 tbsp *chana dhaal*
850 ml/1¹/₂ pints/3¹/₂ cups water
5 tbsp ghee

2 green cardamoms, peeled
4 cloves
8 tbsp sugar
2 tbsp ground almonds
¹/₂ tsp saffron strands
50 g/1³/₄ oz/¹/₄ cup sultanas

1 To make the *pooris*, place the semolina, flour and salt in a bowl and mix. Add the ghee and rub in with your fingers. Add the milk and mix to form a dough. Knead the dough for 5 minutes, cover and leave to rise for about 3 hours. Knead the dough on a floured surface for 15 minutes.

2 Roll out the dough until it measures 25 cm/10 inches and divide into ten portions. Roll out each of these into 12.5 cm/5 inch circles and set aside.

3 To make the filling, soak the *chana dhaal* for at least 3 hours if time allows. Place the *dhaal* in a pan and add 750 ml/1¹/₂ pints water. Bring to the boil over a medium heat until all of the water has evaporated and the *dhaal* is soft enough to be mashed into a paste.

4 In a separate saucepan, heat the ghee and add the cardamom seeds and cloves. Reduce the heat, add the *chana dhaal* paste and stir, scraping the bottom of the pan, for 5-7 minutes.

5 Fold in the sugar and almonds and cook, stirring, for 10 minutes. Add the saffron and sultanas and blend until thickened, stirring, for 5 minutes.

6 Spoon the filling on to one half of each pastry round. Dampen the edges with water and fold the other half over to seal.

7 Heat the ghee in a pan and fry the filled *pooris* over a low heat until golden. Transfer the *pooris* to paper towels, drain and serve.

Indian Bread Pudding

*This, the Indian equivalent of the English bread and butter pudding, is rather
a special dessert, usually cooked for weddings or other special occasions.*

Serves 4-6

INGREDIENTS

6 medium slices bread
5 tbsp ghee (preferably pure)
10 tbsp sugar
300 ml/^{1}/$_2$ pint/1^1/$_4$ cups water
3 green cardamoms, without husks

600 ml/1 pint/2^1/$_2$ cups milk
175 ml/6 fl oz/^{3}/$_4$ cup evaporated
  milk or *khoya* (see Cook's Tip)
^{1}/$_2$ tsp saffron strands

TO DECORATE:
8 pistachio nuts, soaked, peeled and
  chopped
chopped almonds
2 leaves *varq* (silver leaf) (optional)

1 Cut the bread slices into quarters.

2 Heat the ghee in a frying-pan (skillet) and fry the bread slices, turning once, until a crisp golden brown colour.

3 Place the fried bread in the bottom of a heatproof dish and set aside.

4 To make a syrup, place the sugar, water and cardamom seeds in a pan and bring to the boil until the syrup thickens.

5 Pour the syrup over the fried bread.

6 In a separate pan, bring the milk, evaporated milk or *khoya* (see Cook's Tip) and the saffron to the boil over a low heat until the milk has halved in volume.

7 Pour the milk over the syrup-coated bread.

8 Decorate with the pistachios, chopped almonds and *varq* (if using). Serve the bread pudding with or without cream.

COOK'S TIP

To make khoya, *bring 900 ml/
1^1/$_2$ pints of milk to the boil in a
large, heavy saucepan, watching the
milk carefully so that it doesn't
burn. Reduce the heat and boil for
35-40 minutes, stirring
occasionally. The milk should
reduce to a quarter of its volume,
and when completely cooked should
resemble a sticky dough.*

Almond Sherbert

*I prefer to use whole almonds rather than ready-ground almonds
for this dish as I find they give it a better texture.*

Serves 2

INGREDIENTS

225 g/8 oz/2 cups whole almonds
2 tbsp sugar

300 ml/^{1}/$_2$ pint/1^1/$_4$ cups milk

300 ml/^{1}/$_2$ pint/1^1/$_4$ cups water

1 Soak the almonds in a bowl of water for at least 3 hours or preferably overnight.

2 Using a sharp knife, chop the almonds into small pieces. Grind to a fine paste in a food processor or pestle and mortar.

3 Add the sugar to the almond paste and grind once again to form a fine paste.

4 Add the milk and water and mix well (in a liquidizer if you have one).

5 Transfer the almond sherbert to a large serving dish.

6 Leave the almond sherbert to chill in the refrigerator for about 30 minutes. Stir the almond sherbert just before serving.

COOK'S TIP

An electric coffee grinder or spice mill will greatly cut down the time taken to grind the almonds. If using a coffee grinder that is also used for coffee, always remember to clean the grinder thoroughly afterwards, otherwise you will end up with strange-tasting coffee! A pestle and mortar will take longer and is not as good for large quantities.

COOK'S TIP

In India, ice-cool sherberts such as this one are served on special occasions, such as religious festivals. They would be served on the very finest tableware and decorated with varq, the edible silver or gold leaf.

Coconut Sweet

Quick and easy to make, this sweet is very similar to coconut ice.
Pink food colouring may be added towards the end if desired.

Serves 4-6

INGREDIENTS

75 g/2³/4 oz/6 tbsp butter
200 g/7 oz/3 cups desiccated
(shredded) coconut

175 ml/6 fl oz/³/4 cup condensed
milk

a few drops of pink food colouring
(optional)

1 Place the butter in a heavy-based saucepan and melt over a low heat, stirring so that the butter doesn't burn on the bottom of the pan.

2 Add the desiccated coconut to the melted butter, stirring to mix.

3 Stir in the condensed milk and the pink food colouring (if using) and mix continuously for 7-10 minutes.

4 Remove the saucepan from the heat, set aside and leave the coconut mixture to cool slightly.

5 Once cool enough to handle, shape the coconut mixture into long blocks and cut into equal-sized rectangles. Leave to set for about 1 hour, then serve.

COOK'S TIP

Coconut is used extensively in Indian cooking to add flavour and creaminess to various dishes. The best flavour comes from freshly grated coconut, although ready-prepared dessicated (shredded) coconut, as used here, makes an excellent stand-by. Freshly grated coconut freezes successfully, so it is well worth preparing when you have the time.

VARIATION

If you prefer, you could divide the coconut mixture in step 2, and add the pink food colouring to only one half of the mixture. This way, you will have an attractive combination of pink and white coconut sweets.

Semolina Dessert

This dish is eaten with Pooris (see page 236) and Potato Curry (see page 116) for breakfast in northern India. If you like you can serve it with fresh cream for a delicious dessert.

Serves 4

INGREDIENTS

6 tbsp pure ghee
3 whole cloves
3 whole cardamoms
8 tbsp coarse semolina
$^1/_2$ tsp saffron

50 g/1$^3/_4$ oz/$^1/_2$ cup sultanas
10 tbsp sugar
300 ml/$^1/_2$ pint/1$^1/_4$ cups water
300 ml/$^1/_2$ pint/1$^1/_4$ cups milk
cream, to serve

TO DECORATE:
25 g/1 oz/$^1/_2$ cup desiccated
  (shredded) coconut, toasted
25 g/1 oz/$^1/_4$ cup chopped almonds
25 g/1 oz/$^1/_4$ cup pistachio nuts,
  soaked and chopped (optional)

1 Place the ghee in a saucepan and melt over a medium heat.

2 Add the cloves and the whole cardamoms to the melted butter and reduce the heat, stirring to mix.

3 Add the semolina to the mixture in the pan and stir-fry until it turns a little darker.

4 Add the saffron, sultanas and the sugar to the semolina mixture, stirring to mix well.

5 Pour in the water and milk and stir-fry the mixture continuously until the semolina has softened. Add more water if required.

6 Remove the pan from the heat and transfer the semolina to a serving dish.

7 Decorate the semolina dessert with the toasted desiccated (shredded) coconut, flaked almonds and pistachios. Serve with a little cream drizzled over the top.

COOK'S TIP

Cloves are used to give flavour and aroma to both sweet and savoury dishes, but should be used with caution because the flavour can be overwhelming if too many are used.

Carrot Dessert

This makes a very impressive dinner-party dessert. It is best served warm, with fresh cream if desired, and can be made well in advance because it freezes very well.

Serves 4-6

INGREDIENTS

1.5 kg/3 lb 5 oz carrots
10 tbsp ghee
600 ml/1 pint/2¹/₂ pints milk
175 ml/6 fl oz/³/₄ cup evaporated
  milk or *khoya* (see page 238)

10 whole cardamoms, peeled and
  crushed
8-10 tbsp sugar

TO DECORATE:
25 g/1 oz/¹/₄ cup pistachio nuts,
  chopped
2 leaves *varq* (silver leaf) (optional)

1 Rinse, peel and grate the carrots.

2 Heat the ghee in a large, heavy saucepan.

3 Add the grated carrots to the ghee and stir-fry for 15-20 minutes or until the moisture from the carrots has evaporated and the carrots have darkened in colour.

4 Add the milk, evaporated milk or *khoya*, cardamoms and sugar to the carrot mixture and continue to stir-fry for a further 30-35 minutes, until it is a rich brownish-red colour.

5 Transfer the carrot mixture to a large shallow dish.

6 Decorate with the pistachio nuts and *varq* (if using) and serve at once.

COOK'S TIP

A quicker way to grate the carrots is to use a food processor.

COOK'S TIP

I like to use pure ghee for this dessert as it is rather special and tastes better made with pure ghee. However, if you are trying to limit your fat intake, use vegetable ghee instead.

Sweet Saffron Rice

*This is a traditional dessert which is quick and easy to make and looks
very impressive, especially decorated with pistachio nuts and* varq *(silver leaf).*

Serves 4

INGREDIENTS

200 g/7 oz/1 cup basmati rice
200 g/7 oz/1 cup sugar
1 pinch saffron strands
300 ml/^{1}/$_2$ pint/1^1/$_4$ cups water

2 tbsp ghee
3 cloves
3 cardamoms
25 g/1 oz/2 tbsp sultanas

TO DECORATE:
a few pistachio nuts (optional)
varq (silver leaf) (optional)

1 Rinse the rice twice and bring to the boil in a saucepan of water, stirring. Remove the pan from the heat when the rice is half-cooked, drain the rice thoroughly and set aside.

2 In a separate saucepan, boil the sugar and saffron in the water, stirring, until the syrup thickens. Set the syrup aside until required.

3 In another saucepan, heat the ghee, cloves and cardamoms, stirring occasionally. Remove the pan from the heat.

4 Return the rice to a low heat and add the sultanas, stirring to combine.

5 Pour the syrup over the rice mixture and stir to mix.

6 Pour the ghee mixture over the rice and leave to simmer over a low heat for 10-15 minutes. Check to see whether the rice is cooked; if not, add a little water, cover and leave to simmer.

7 Serve warm, decorated with pistachio nuts and *varq* (silver leaf), and with cream if desired.

VARIATION

For a slightly stronger saffron flavour, place the saffron strands on a small piece of kitchen foil and toast them lightly under a hot grill (broiler) for a few moments (take care not to overcook them or the flavour will spoil) and crush finely between your fingers before adding to the sugar and water in step 2.

Ground Almonds Cooked in Ghee & Milk

Traditionally served at breakfast in India, this almond-based dish is said to sharpen the mind!
However, it can be served as a delicious dessert and is very quick to make.

Serves 2-4

INGREDIENTS

2 tbsp vegetable or pure ghee
25 g/1 oz/¼ cup plain (all-purpose) flour

100 g/3½ oz/½ cup ground almonds
300 ml/½ pint/1¼ cups milk

50 g/1¾ oz/¼ cup sugar
fresh mint leaves, to decorate

1 Place the ghee in a small, heavy-based saucepan. Melt the ghee over a gentle heat, stirring so that it doesn't burn.

2 Reduce the heat and add the flour, stirring vigorously to remove any lumps.

3 Add the almonds to the ghee and flour mixture, stirring continuously.

4 Gradually add the milk and sugar to the mixture in the pan and bring to the boil. Continue cooking for 3-5 minutes or until the liquid is smooth and reaches the consistency of cream of chicken soup.

5 Transfer to a serving dish, decorate and serve hot.

COOK'S TIP

Ghee comes in two forms and can be bought from Asian grocers. It is worth noting that pure ghee, made from melted butter, is not suitable for vegans, although there is a vegetable ghee available from Indian grocers and some health-food stores.

VARIATION

You could use coconut milk in this recipe, for a delicious alternative.

Indian Vermicelli Pudding

Indian vermicelli (seviyan), which is very fine, is delicious cooked in milk and ghee. Muslims make this for one of their religious festivals called Eid, *which is celebrated at the end of Ramadan.*

Serves 4–6

INGREDIENTS

25 g/1 oz pistachio nuts (optional)
25 g/1 oz flaked almonds
3 tbsp ghee

100 g/3¹/₂ oz/1¹/₂ cups *seviyan*
(Indian vermicelli)
850 ml/1¹/₂ pints/3¹/₂ cups milk

175 ml/6 fl oz/³/₄ cup evaporated
milk
8 tbsp sugar
6 dates, stoned and dried

1 Soak the pistachio nuts (if using) in a bowl of water for at least 3 hours. Peel the pistachios and mix them with the flaked almonds. Chop the nuts finely and set aside.

2 Melt the ghee in a large saucepan and lightly fry the *seviyan* (Indian vermicelli). Reduce the heat immediately (the *seviyan* will turn golden brown very quickly so be careful not to burn it), and if necessary remove the pan from the heat (do not worry if some bits are a little darker than others).

3 Add the milk to the *seviyan* (Indian vermicelli) and bring to the boil slowly, taking care that it does not boil over.

4 Add the evaporated milk, sugar and the stoned dates to the mixture in the pan. Leave to simmer for about 10 minutes, uncovered, stirring occasionally. When the consistency starts to thicken, pour the pudding into a serving bowl.

5 Decorate the pudding with the chopped pistachio nuts and flaked almonds.

COOK'S TIP

You will find seviyan *(Indian vermicelli) in Indian grocers. This dessert can be served warm or cold.*

Almond & Pistachio Dessert

Rich and mouth-watering, this dessert can be prepared in advance of the meal. It is best served cold.

Serves 4–6

INGREDIENTS

75 g/2³/₄ oz/6 tbsp unsalted butter
200 g/7 oz/1 cup ground almonds
200 g/7 oz/1 cup sugar

150 ml/5 fl oz/²/₃ cup single (light) cream
8 almonds, chopped

10 pistachio nuts, chopped

1 Place the butter in a medium-sized saucepan, preferably non-stick. Melt the butter, stirring well.

2 Add the ground almonds, cream and sugar to the melted butter in the pan, stirring to combine. Reduce the heat and stir constantly for 10-12 minutes, scraping the bottom of the pan.

3 Increase the heat until the mixture turns a little darker in colour.

4 Transfer the almond mixture to a shallow serving dish and smooth the top with the back of a spoon.

5 Decorate the top of the dessert with the chopped almonds and pistachios.

6 Leave the dessert to set for about 1 hour, then cut into diamond shapes and serve cold.

COOK'S TIP

This almond dessert can be made in advance and stored in an airtight container in the refrigerator for several days.

COOK'S TIP

You could use a variety of shaped pastry cutters, to cut the dessert into different shapes, rather than diamonds, if you prefer.

Index

Index compiled by Hilary Bird.